T0132160

The Prayer Letters

MARIE WATTERS-BROWN

iUniverse, Inc.
New York   Bloomington

iUniverse books may be ordered through booksellers or by contacting:

iUniverse
1663 Liberty Drive
Bloomington, IN 47403
www.iuniverse.com
1-800-Authors (1-800-288-4677)

ISBN: 978-1-4401-8664-6 (sc)
ISBN: 978-1-4401-8663-9 (ebook)

Library of Congress Control Number: 2009911757

Printed in the United States of America

iUniverse rev. date: 11/12/2009

"More things are wrought by prayer than this world dreams of."
Alfred Lord Tennyson

My immeasurable gratitude to my husband, Ian, who is my loving supporter of all things, and to my daughters Megan and Taylore for their love and belief in me and my works. Applause to Bill, my computer genius, and Marty, my blessed encourager.

Contents

Introduction

Letter writing has been my personal indulgence. I have been writing letters for so long that I cannot recall when I began. I often awake with a letter happening in my head to someone for whom I have a message. When I am unable to relax, the only relief seems to be to donate my jumbled thoughts to paper. Once that is accomplished, I creep back to bed and relax into sleep.

At the peak of my letter writing, I frequently found myself caught up in the personal lives of friends and acquaintances and their recurring hurts and disappointments. One of my greatest gifts is that I am a good listener, and I believe that conversation is a great healer. My friends and family know that if they need to talk to someone today, they can just call me and receive my undivided attention. I instantly take on a sincere concern that they find themselves into a happy solution. I become totally involved in their needs and am committed to helping them heal from the moment they begin talking.

I love challenges, and I love finding solutions. I am interested in what makes people "tick." A banal expression, but that's really it. I just finished reading Peter Gzowski's *The Private Voice*. I hung on every word. It is all about all the interviews he has done, the questions he has asked, the replies he has received, and the observations he has made.

Each of my interactions was so different from any other and so fascinating. When people came to me to talk, I got an enviable peek into their workings. I always promised to pray after we talked because they were looking for help, and I felt obligated to speed each one toward relief. Prayer has always been the solution to my personal dilemmas, my fears, my pain, and my confusion. I discovered the power of prayer and its comforting and life-changing results when I was eleven years old. These letters are the answers to prayers and the resolutions that came to me in various ways. People changed; I also changed, and I am grateful.

For those of you who will read this book, I wonder what your story would be and how miracles could happen for you. I wonder what you saw on the cover or thumbing through the chapters that led you to take a copy of this book home. Perhaps your story is in here somewhere. If it is, you may find a thread of relief from a soul like yourself. Of course, I have changed the names and other identifying factors of those to whom I have written to protect their privacy. I share this correspondence with you because I have been asked to do so. Often, when someone was the recipient of a letter, the response would be, "You should write a book." So here we are.

1
The Grace of God

Dear Reader,

A week ago, after a conversation with my pastor about a number of things, he asked me to give a testimonial at the two morning services. Although I am an experienced public speaker, I was somewhat fainthearted to be speaking formally to so many friends.

The following is what I said:

"Teaching was my second career, and I loved every moment of it. I loved that I could watch people change their lives. I knew teaching was my gift from God and my calling. It was invigorating, challenging, and satisfying. However, the glitch in my career was a corrupt principal who was involved in unspeakable activities. Students came to me to do something about his behavior, so he knew that I knew. He badgered me about incidentals; he kept close tabs on me and made things uncomfortable for me at work, until one day I went to his office and resigned right in the middle of a huge teacher layoff. Still, I knew I had done the right thing. I walked back to my classroom in tears, angry and desolate, and was overheard to say, 'I'll start my own damn school!'

"Ten years later, that is exactly what I did. During the preceding two years, I prayed for guidance and wisdom to do it God's way, to teach what was needed, and to find the right environment and the patience to deal with certain powers. I was a single parent who was supporting three children entirely on my own and preparing to embark on a huge adventure. The interesting thing is that I was never afraid. I knew I was meant to do this. It was clear that God was leading me, and as the plan grew, I could see a unique place of learning developing. During those two years, I hired myself out to a variety of businesses and professions, told them of my plan, and asked what qualities they wanted most in those they would hire. I often worked for the president of the company in the capacity of confidential or private secretary. They were thrilled that someone would approach them and were very forthcoming. I filled my books with notes, and it was through that experience that the curriculum was developed.

"In September 1975, the Halifax Business Academy was founded. I was the sole owner, and I dubbed myself president. I was unknown to the public; however, the confidence that arose from my prayers kept me courageous and firm about the plan. I remortgaged my home; made a payment on a red brick building in downtown Halifax; borrowed twenty-five thousand dollars from the bank for furniture, equipment, and advertising; and dove in. At the beginning of September, we had registered twenty-five students in a ten-month program. In January, we added a six-month program. In June, we graduated sixty-five students. I had an emergency plan, however. All our desks were constructed to be converted to tables for a restaurant if no one showed up. Never give up, said I.

"The Academy outgrew its first building, expanded into a new and larger location, grew some more, and moved into an old broadcasting house in the center of the city. By then, we were graduating a total of six hundred students a year in full-time and part-time programs. We were the largest and most recognized business training center in Atlantic Canada. We deposited one million dollars in the bank every September, and it carried us through the year. A study conducted by the Institute of Public Affairs of Dalhousie University revealed that the Academy boasted the highest employability rate of any institution of learning in Nova Scotia. Ninety-five percent of the students were guaranteed employment within one month of graduation.

"We were recognized by major companies and several universities. Many of our students came in with bachelor's and master's degrees. Our success was the result of several things: fourteen exceptional, dedicated staff members who promised to teach with love; original courses current with business and industry and the professions, such as medicine, law, banking, engineering, and education in the development of a healthy body, mind, and spirit supported by prayer. We prayed in the staff room for guidance and wisdom and patience, and we prayed in the classroom according to requests from the students. Some students experienced prayer for the first time. The Academy was alive with joy and confidence, and gratitude and continued to grow.

"*Until* one awful day nearly twenty years later.

"We had entered into a contract with the owner of our new building to pay rent of fourteen thousand dollars per month and at the end of three years to purchase the building. The building needed improvements in the amount of $350,000. Our banker told us to proceed with the work, paying as it was completed, and then return to the bank for a ten-year mortgage, which they would carry. We did just that. We completed the work, paid all the bills, and returned to the bank with $350,000 less in our account. However, there was a new manager, and he refused to honor the contract. He was terribly patronizing, found me amusing, and suggested I shut down and 'get a nice job as someone's secretary.' I knew this was sexism, but I pressed on. While I was angry and frustrated, I believed there was a solution because of our valid financial status. The banker did agree to a line of credit of $150,000 to get us through until September when the account would be full again. I was required to guarantee my waterfront property and my car. I felt no risk, but actually, I had no choice.

"I was encouraged to go to the minister of development with my request for the ten-year mortgage. I did so, accompanied by my accountant, my lawyer, and my husband. The minister was encouraging on the first meeting, telling us how proud he was of the Academy and how the province would certainly support us as we had been saving them substantial costs annually by training productive, working taxpayers instead of adding to the unemployed. He set the wheels in motion after numerous meetings with his advisors. A check for $350,000 was to be delivered on August 1 before noon. He said to us on our last visit two weeks before: 'We never break promises. You shall have your money.' But at noon, there was no check.

"I called his office. His secretary said he was on holiday. I advised her that I would give him one hour, and I was going to the press. Instead, a letter from the minister arrived with the message that there would be no financing of a mortgage. No explanation. No apology. The following morning, the owner of the building was standing on the front steps with his lawyer. He had locked the doors. He already knew. I told him I could deliver the rent in full in two weeks, but he would not budge. He gave the staff and me twenty-four hours to remove our personal belongings from the building. We emptied the files into garbage bags, and I took them home. All the thousands of dollars' worth of furniture and equipment were to remain. The bank expedited the selling of our home and car to satisfy the line of credit. I had used all my personal savings to support the Academy.

"Within two weeks we learned from colleagues in Province House that the owner of our building was a relative and friend of the minister of development. This minister arranged for the owner to get his building back to help him weather a financial crisis. In doing so, he harmed those students registered for September's term (one month away) who had already paid rent on apartments. I wrote to each of them personally during the summer and returned their registration fees, which were always held in trust. I told them the truth. I was interviewed by every newspaper, television station, and radio station and I told them the truth. Three ministers from the province called me privately to express their condolences and to tell me they knew what was happening but could do nothing about it.

"Too soon, another crisis. My husband's partner robbed him of his investments in a partnership, locked the doors, and fled town. We felt as though we had been shot. I cannot describe the emotions. Anger, frustration, helplessness. We were devastated and very frightened.

We had no place to live and no money for food or gas. We placed all our belongings and furniture into storage and looked for a place to sleep. With credit enough for one month's worth of expenses on our American Express Card, we checked into a grungy motel for one month with our two little poodles, where we existed on soup and Kraft dinners.

"My husband and I prayed day and night. We fell into one another's arms and prayed. We prayed to understand how this terrible thing had happened and to know what to do next. We—two honest, busy, industrious business people—had no work, no income, and no plan. We talked. We prayed. We prayed for sleep and peace and opportunity. While the pain and fear pursued us, a wonderful thing was happening. We got to know one another. As we sat together to pray, we held hands and prayed out loud. We heard what was in the other's heart, and we grew to love one another more each day. We each discovered the wonderful person that the other was. As we listened to the other pray, we learned the other's truth. No one lies to God. As you can see, we have survived, and we are proud of the way we have conquered the fears, the anger, and the regret, and slowly—very slowly—we have forgiven.

"In the early days, to remind myself that there was hope in the midst of our losses, I prayed: 'The Lord is my Shepherd, I shall not want, I shall not want, I shall not want.'

"I could not just sit and grieve, and my eyes had run out of tears. So, I discovered walking. I walked six miles a day. I walked so much that I actually wore out my boots. And as I walked, I repeated: 'The Lord is my Shepherd, I shall not want.' I walked through parks; I sat by the ocean.

"My Lord made me to lie down in green pastures; he led me beside the still waters. He restored my soul. He led me in the paths of righteousness. As time passed, I felt that I had passed through the valley of the shadow of death. My fears diminished.

"Now, on this day, you can see that Ian and I have recovered and have developed more wisdom, courage, and patience. We have enough of everything—a life of joy and peace and days of ongoing miracles. We can say truly that 'our cup runneth over.' We are overflowing with gratitude, and I thank God daily for my beloved husband.

"Two elderly people have rebuilt their lives, experience gratitude every morning, experience joy every day, and experience peaceful rest every night. We have a perfect, although modest, home that welcomes the birds to our window. We have a nest in a warmer climate where we spend our winters, and we have a magical relationship. We have good health and good friends and loving children. The world is unfolding as it should."

Marie Watters-Brown

2

On Loneliness

Dear Sally,

Today's visit was nice, as always. I am happy to spend time with you, and I bask in your compliments, which are so generous. I accept them because I know you are sincere. If somehow I have enriched your life, it is because you deserve it, and God knows that and gives me the means to say or do what he wants you to hear. I am just a voice.

I told you I would pray for you. And I did. As I was lying there in the quiet last night, I asked God to come to you. I asked him to find a way to make you receptive. I dozed off and awoke with the desire to write to you. So here I am.

You asked why God has forsaken you. He has not done that. More likely, you have forsaken yourself. When we feel forsaken, sometimes it is because we have not used all our own resources to change our lives.

You said you are very lonely. Yet, you are surrounded by people who care. Everyone has bouts of loneliness. It is a part of the thread of life. It often cannot be relieved by the presence of others; they often bring their own loneliness with them. It seems that the loneliness comes from an eternal search for an elusive internal part of ourselves—I call that the God connection. We feel alone. When we have good days, we feel happy; we focus on pleasure and beauty. When the difficult days come along, we forget about the beauty that is still there waiting to be noticed once again.

I have a devoted husband who is with me all the time, living in harmony, laughing together, sharing a lovely life. Yet, I, too, experience loneliness. It seems to appear when I have separated myself from God for a time. Now when I have that sense of longing for something and can't identify what it is, or I feel the need for people, instead of heading for the telephone to engage in chatter as I might once have done, I sit in my favorite chair by the window, close my eyes, do a bit of deep breathing, and meditate on all the blessings in my life—my soft chair, my cozy home, my warm coffee, my valued friends, my dear little shih tzu, my precious children, my loyal husband, and so much more. I go into prayer and express gratitude for all my blessings. As I do this, the list gets longer, and I become aware of a filling up. I know the Holy Spirit is filling me and opening my senses to how fortunate I am. I spend some time praying for others, and soon the loneliness has vanished.

So many people have difficulty with silence. On request, I created a meditation CD for a group of women. Many have expressed their gratitude, as they find it a great aid in changing their habits. It is called "Finding Your Quiet Place." What is amazing about it is that some have expressed relief from physical pain. Some have experienced peaceful sleep. If you would like one, I will send it to you, and with my blessing.

Much love,

Marie

3
Loving an Unlovable Mother

Dear Jenny,

I have just hung up the phone, and while it may be presumptuous on my part to write you a letter about these difficult times, I am doing it anyway, because my motives are pure. As I said on the phone, I have been through it all. I have experienced all the terrible things one could imagine and have recovered completely from some and substantially from others.

This could be a long epistle. Take a cup of tea to the soft seat near that window that shows you God's good earth.

I shall share with you one experience that we have in common—our relationships with our mothers. It ruled my life and resulted in bad choices of the men in my life. I believe now that it might even have cost me all my worldly goods. That is pretty shocking, but after years of introspection, I know there is a connection between one of the saddest and most challenging times in my life and the messages I got from my mother. Please understand that I do not blame her. I think she often did the best she knew how to do.

Many of the hurts were not intentional. They came out of the disappointments and pain from her own life. Others came from upbringing.

I tell you this so you will understand my views. I pray about everything. I started praying when I was eleven years old. We were members of the Anglican Church as a family, although not at all devout. We attended church every Sunday, however, and because the service is ritual, I committed it to memory. To this day, if I cannot sleep at night, I repeat the entire Holy Communion service over and over. There is a prayer of confession that releases stresses that have accumulated and thoughts and deeds that I regret.

During my childhood, my parents fought regularly and in very loud voices. It was frightening and terribly painful. My mother would goad my father into losing his temper. I recognized the pattern and found it confusing. I did not understand why she behaved that way; I only knew I would never shout at anyone. To this day, I have difficulty shouting, even when I should.

I was an only child—an adopted child. We lived two miles from the nearest family, on a large farm, on a point of land, surrounded by water. It was wonderful with trees of all varieties and lots of apple trees. When the noise started in the house and I felt bewildered, I would race to the orchard, lie down under an apple tree, and say the Lord's Prayer. I just knew I was being heard. I had a less-than-vague conception of God, but I knew I was being heard, and I always felt better afterward. So I developed a life of prayer. Prayer has saved my life and brought me physical healing, emotional peace, mental clarity, and spiritual depth. With all these great gifts, I have much to share. I am blessed, and I am grateful. And I am available to you. You take nothing from me. Whatever I give is always returned tenfold.

My mother was eighty-nine when she died, and I was fifty-eight. I was as vulnerable to her as a five-year-old whenever she criticized me. Praise and acceptance were rare in my lifetime with her, and she only once said "I love you." She was shouting it at the time. Her criticisms covered everything: my housekeeping, my cooking, my hairdo and dress style, my friends, and my parenting. I tried so hard to seek her approval and to bring pleasure to her face. I was never successful. She hated the men in my life and, more than that, found my marriages a source of shame. Ironically, my faulty choices of partners were directly related to the emptiness I bore from the lack of her love.

I just wanted to be loved. That was all. I spent my life looking for someone to fill the void. She would not have understood any of that, and we never discussed my lifelong emptiness. She was, nevertheless, a conscientious mother. I was not neglected. She took care to see that I was healthy, well fed, and safe. The hurt is gone now. I am healed, but I still remember, although less clearly.

On Mother's Day Sunday some years ago, she and I were in church, and she was kneeling for prayer. I had a sudden awareness of how tiny she was, how fragile, and that we had only a few years left to become close. I knew if that were to happen, it would be my responsibility to work toward that. I did not know then that she had only three years left. I did not know, but I sensed it. I began praying diligently for guidance. What could I do to change things? What did she need from me? *Lord, tell me what to do.* I prayed daily—in the morning, in the evening, and at times in between. I awoke one morning at four o'clock with a mountain of emotions and images that played in my head like a film, on and on. They were all of my mother and me. My head was alive with internal conversation. I got out of bed, went to the kitchen table, grabbed an old notebook and pencil, and began to write. I wrote what I had been "dreaming." Thought followed thought almost faster than I could record. I wrote for four hours. I wept and wept and sweated through my flannelette pajamas. I filled the book. Then I read it through several times.

It was revealed to me that inside that grown eighty-six-year-old woman was a hurting little girl. I understood right away that I was to assume the role of her mother, to love her unconditionally, to discipline her, to show leadership, and to make some rules.

I took her to lunch at least once a week, but never on the same day, so we would not build a pattern. I always took her somewhere she enjoyed. When she began complaining, instead of crumpling inside, I would tell her that I brought her out to spend time with her and to enjoy her company and that it spoiled our time when she complained. I could see her surprise. I never raised my voice. I never got annoyed. I was just calm and firm. Years ago, I would have asked her why she was always so critical, what had I done wrong, inviting a fresh barrage of negativity. This was different. I was guided.

I called her often by phone, and we would chat about domestic things—what she had been doing, how she was feeling, what I had been doing. A nice chat would eventually develop into her barrage of what was wrong with me. I told her she was making me feel sad again and that it was probably time to hang up now, which I did.

I often took her driving when I had appointments just to get her out somewhere, and then we would have lunch together. One day she got in the car, and before we had gone a block, she started. First it was my awful hairdo, then where did I get the outfit, then idle comments about the ugliness of some innocent woman out walking. I turned the car around and stopped at her door. I told her I had invited her driving to have a pleasant time together, and because this was not happening, I was taking her home. She was boiling and said she would never speak to me again. I replied that it was her choice, but I had done nothing to deserve this behavior, and when she was ready to treat me well, she should call. I said all this in a calm voice, but my heart was beating a hole in my chest. Meanwhile, I was praying.

Six months passed. It was a long six months, because the little girl in me was afraid of what she would do or say next. The grown woman in me, however, began to enjoy a certain relief. My son asked me to promise I would not call her. "She will call you," he said. "This is a good thing." Sure enough, one day the phone rang, and she talked as though we had been in touch yesterday. We had a nice, long chat, and then it began to deteriorate. I said, "Great to hear from you mother; we'll talk soon, but I must go," and I hung up.

I continued that pattern every time she called as soon as the conversation turned mean. She began to change. We developed a nice friendship as we went to lunch, went shopping, or just visited together. I hugged her if she would permit me and told her I loved her. She was unable to respond but had become quite respectful and more pleasant regarding the other facets of her life. I gave her all the time she needed to complain about her aging body and its constraints and encouraged her as I knew how.

She died at age eighty-nine of pneumonia and heart failure. I was with her to her last hour and often told her I loved her. I wanted to stay with her and hold her hand, but she asked me to leave. We did not have the happy ending I would have liked, but it had resolution for me. That is what you need, my friend, just for you—resolution and peace.

You cannot provoke happiness in your mother. She has her own misery and, for whatever reason, has never dealt with it or attempted healing. Few of us pass through this planet without our dragons. The deepest hurts are the oldest ones, beginning in childhood. Your mother probably has lots of them. She is obviously envious of you, and understandably so. You have a beautiful face and an endearing personality. I am sure you hear that daily from your husband. You have beautiful offspring. As a child, she probably got no attention and no compliments. She has not experienced the pleasure of an admiring mother and so has never become one. Whatever she says to you is probably a projection of her own deepest view of herself. You have overcome a former unhappy marriage and a divorce. You now have a magnificent property, a lovely lifestyle, and a husband who adores you and tells everyone. She would not recognize envy in herself, but it is there big time. She has only her own negative thoughts—regrets, self-criticism, disappointments—to pass on to you.

Whatever you conceive God to be, there is no doubt that one exists. Your husband says he doesn't believe, and yet, he lives as though he does. He plants seeds and tends gardens with faith that all will grow. I believe that whatever we put into the universe comes back to us. If you could substitute a feeling of unconditional love for a feeling of hurt when you connect with her, it would make a difference in how much less hurt you feel. Teach her how to be loving and how to treat you. She either does not know or does not have the moral strength to tell you what you deserve to hear. She sees how your life is and looks at her own and observes a wide gap. So she narrows it by making you feel like less of a person. Now you are a little more alike for a while in her mind. That is how envy works.

The trouble is, her spirit knows what she has done, and she ultimately feels worse instead of better, so she has to take a crack at something else. And on it goes. This understanding has made me very conscious of the words I use with my precious daughters. I tell them the good truths: that they are interesting, beautiful, brave, and accomplished. Those things I observe that I might like to change I do not express unless I am asked, and I am careful how I respond. Your daughter has love in her face when she looks at you, so I presume she gets the support she needs from her mother.

Your mother has not outgrown her childhood pain; she is a victim. She has not worked out her emotional issues. She has not grown or matured. When she is in your home, she is not behaving like an adult while she accepts your hospitality. She says terrible things that paralyze both of you emotionally and has become so good at it that you both you and your husband are afraid of her. That is bizarre, is it not?! Two grown, successful, loving, happy people who are doing good things with their lives and are admired and respected by their children and friends are afraid of a small woman who appears in their lives only three weeks out of fifty-two. Worse still, not a day will go by this year that thoughts will not pass through your mind. You will experience moments of sadness and frustration; you will talk about it a little, promise to leave it alone, and then one day take it out and do it all again. I know. I lived it. Don't let this happen to you.

My mother convinced me my failed marriages were my fault, albeit both men were problem drinkers (and that was only the visible problem). Most of me knew it was not my fault, but some of me gave in to the possibility, and it haunted me. I fought her opinions of me, but they did their damage.

What we are afraid of is that if we speak up, it will get worse, and we can't deal with that. I was a successful businesswoman with a renowned business college. My students thought I had the courage to face anything. Imagine if I had announced to all eight hundred of them at a graduation exercise that I was terrified of my mother, allowed her to be abusive, and never confronted her.

My solution was to pray, asking what I needed to do to make things right for her and for me. You need to do that, too. You will get answers, your head will begin to clear, and you will build resolve. You will feel determination. One day an opportunity will arise, and it will be a perfect moment to do or say what you need to. Tell her in your own kind way what the new rules are. Do it quietly and lovingly. Don't ask her why she behaves as she does. Don't give her an opportunity to tell you what is wrong with you. Just tell her how things will be from now on and what you will not permit.

Remember the old childhood refrain: "Sticks and stones will break my bones, but words will never hurt me." Whoever said that was dead wrong. Parents who malign their children at any age, whether they deserve it or not, are neglecting their emotional and spiritual nourishment. They cause lifelong pain and often disease and seriously destructive behavior. Most alcoholic adults are trying to subdue the pain of the aftermath of a hurtful childhood.

Just pray that she will find peace in her heart. Pray that you will find courage and patience. Believe that everything is going to change. Have faith. It happened for me—prayer made it happen. After my first successful encounter with my mother, I felt a small breath of confidence and relief and gratitude. I gave thanks and continued to pray.

If you do what you do with a loving heart and instead of a fearful one, you will make the right decisions for yourself. I guarantee you will see small miracles happen.

Bless you both.

Marie

4
Those Last Hours

Dear Fran and Kale,

I don't know what to say to you. We just want you to know how sorry we are that you are dealing with this shocking prognosis. There are no words to describe how you are feeling, of course, and how you will endure this next short passage of time.

Life is so unpredictable. We have plans, and suddenly, an earthquake occurs. We would like to help but feel helpless. I know you will hear "if there's anything we can do" from lots of people, and although it will be sincere, we are still only spectators.

I am in the sixth week of recovery of open-heart surgery. It was both awful and wonderful. The surgeons have performed miracles, and I have come to realize how lucky I am. The first three weeks were a nightmare, and I would not have had the courage to enter into the procedure had I understood the details of what was about to happen. I am not very brave. However, I appreciate that I have been given an extension on my life. With the knowledge that every day, every hour, is precious, I must do something of value with it. We become wise so late. Ian was been pretty much consumed with looking after me, as I could not be left alone in a room for the first three weeks.

Although we have not been lifelong friends, we like you very much and are overwhelmed by the challenges you will be working through together. It is obvious you have a good relationship, and that is reason for gratitude. I frequently remind Ian how important he is in my life when I consider how different this experience would have been without him. Friends were valiant and wrote notes of comfort. I learned how much I was loved.

There were many nights I lay awake in the dark, unable to move. I found that my only comfort was prayer. I don't know of your beliefs or the extent of your faith, but I would urge you to use those difficult and lonely times for prayer. It takes no skill, and it is as available as the air. I guarantee you will be heard if you seek comfort. Years ago, when my world was plummeting, I used to repeat the twenty-third Psalm over and over, especially the first line: "The Lord is my Shepherd, I shall not want." I found it to have a confirming effect that took the edge off my moments of desperation.

There is no explanation for why some of us are to suffer extraordinarily, while others skate through life seemingly unscathed. In our short life together, Ian and I have been challenged often with illness and significant material losses—all our worldly goods, our home, and our savings were lost in one year. The worst of it was being scavenged by greedy politicians with powerful connections—people we trusted. We, naïve and trusting, did not see it happen. We had a huge mountain to climb just to regain emotional equilibrium.

There was only one source of wisdom and comfort and hope, and that was to turn to prayer. We prayed. Certainly, neither of us has had cancer, so we cannot fit in your shoes. But this we know to be true: we have recovered from every dreadful crisis. We have become more loving as individuals, more optimistic in the goodness in the world, and more confident in an unshakeable faith that can overcome anything because we have prayed.

Our prayers have become effective in remarkable ways since we began praying together, out loud, in the presence of one another. We heard the truth of the other's needs and feelings and fears in the act of praying aloud. We hold hands when we pray. It confirms our connection, our togetherness. The illness belongs to both of you, as you have discovered.

We pray wherever we are when we are in need. We might stop the car for prayer. We pray in bed, at a meal, lying on the beach. We know we are heard, because we have evidence. We don't always get what we ask for, but we always get something invaluable and always what we need. I hope you will pray and will find release and comfort.

There were hundreds of people praying for me during my illness. I knew it. I could feel it. I felt enveloped and protected. I never felt alone. We will be praying for you constantly. Ask people to pray for you. It will bless them as well as you.

May the good Lord hold you in the palm of his hand until we meet again.

Marie and Ian

5

Clarity out of Confusion

Dear Sandy,

Something extraordinary happened at the end of the prayer on Thursday, and I was too overwhelmed to tell you at that moment, but I believe it is important. When I opened my eyes and looked over at you, you looked transparent—that is, you were a silvery color. The only visible features were your eyes. Your eyes were closed, and I saw the shadows of your lashes. I don't mean I could look through you. It is just that the you before the prayer was not what I was seeing. I have never experienced this before. I felt I must not disturb you and that you were in a private place.

You said that you had never felt so peaceful. I thought, however, that we were no longer in the same dimension that we were in an hour before. Was that the presence of the Holy Spirit? I do know about auras, but it did not look like an aura.

I have since prayed for you to be guided and clear minded about what his plans are for you, and what I sense again is that you must take care of yourself. If you take care of yourself, your children will automatically be cared for. I do not know how things will turn out for you and your husband as a couple, but you know you cannot change him. That is his to do.

When I needed relief from any stress, changing myself, my perspective, and my behavior changed both me and Ian. It made me a stronger, wiser person through the prayers and the responses. I know that something important will eventually happen if you pray for your husband. Just pray that he be opened to the guidance and protection of the Holy Spirit, that he be forgiven, and that he be blessed. In praying for blessings for the other, particularly if the other is a problem, I feel released in some way; I no longer feel the need to "fix" him because now it is in the Lord's care.

Try to give up passing judgment on everything he says at the time he is speaking, even though he is the one who has damaged the trust. He may be telling the truth. It doesn't mean you should believe him; just let it pass through you and get on with doing what is right for you. Try not to comment on everything, and as you hear your mind forming opinions, disengage yourself and instead observe if there are any changes in you or in him.

If you can develop a bit of patience and behave with a wait-and-see attitude for a little while, you might have a more accurate understanding of how things really are. He is your partner, not your responsibility. Your goal is to determine if you can overcome your doubts (or if you should) and to work toward a satisfying and productive life for you and your children. As we agree, you need to get out of limbo. Work toward one decision or another. As you pose either/or to yourself, sit quietly and check your solar plexus. See how it "feels" to you.

Don't give up on prayers, but do give up praying casually to the clouds. Try to place yourself in the presence of the Holy Spirit each time so that you will have a strong sense of yourself in his presence and a strong sense of truth at that time. Truth is all that matters. The rest will fall into place. When we are "in the spirit" rather than "in the ego," we are moving in the truth. The ego asserts itself to get its own way according to habit or old conditioning. The spirit places us in a positive, loving attitude.

Because God is love, there is no fear when we move in his will.

If you need to talk more, ask. I am always available. Conversation is clarifying. You need to hear your voice saying what your mind has been thinking. The mind gets like a can of spaghetti sometimes—no order, just an accumulation of confusion with no results. I will always have time for you. This is how I serve. I listen, and then I pray, and then I communicate.

God's blessings on you,

Marie

6
The Sky's the Limit

Dear Alla and Clay,

You have been in my thoughts often since our unusual encounter in a Vancouver coffee shop. When I asked two strangers to share a table, who could imagine we would experience an extraordinary event?

While I was drinking my coffee, I was moved by Alla's beauty and was curious to know who you were. I knew you were unique. You were beautifully dressed with wonderful style. I felt quite envious of your youth and vitality. Then we got to talking about fashion in Russia and fashion in Canada. I was thinking that I wished I were svelter and had chosen something chic to wear that day.

When I discovered that you are a concert pianist, I suddenly felt strange, as though I had walked into a play, as though I were playing a role, and I had no idea what it was. The next moment, you asked to play for me, and I found myself whisked away to your home for a private concert. As we were getting in the car, it occurred to me that I should perhaps be more concerned for my safety. After all, we were total strangers only ten minutes ago. Yet, I felt peaceful and confident and just knew that I was safe and that something extraordinary was about to happen.

Alla, I was completely swept away by your music. When I closed my eyes, I was in a concert hall, and you were in a beautiful gown; the music was beyond description. I cannot thank you enough. You gave me a gift that day, and I shall treasure it always. A moment carved out of time and framed in my mind forever. As I said that day, it was no coincidence that we met and spent that time as we did. I was honored, and I believe it is because in some way I was to honor you.

I am a woman of deep spiritual belief and try to follow a Christian lifestyle. I told you that I believe prayer is powerful and that we get answers when we pray. We must pray with a fervent heart and a confident belief that God will answer. My life is an answer to prayers. Miracles happen daily, and you were my miracle that day. Perhaps I am simply a messenger for you.

I have been home since Tuesday recovering from jet lag. I told you both I would pray for you, and I have been. Some things have come through for each of you individually and probably for both of you as a couple. This is what I have been sensing so far.

I would love it if you both wrote to me. Do not worry about the quality of your English. Your spoken English is remarkable, and your accent is charming. I, unfortunately, don't know Russian at all. I am trying to improve my French because we took a trip to Paris last June. My husband flew me there for a birthday surprise. It was thrilling, as I toured all the great art galleries, walked through the streets of the city, and munched on croissants at sidewalk cafes.

Clay, I recognize that you are frustrated now with your lack of work. You need to work. We all do. Work is our way of saying thank you to God for his gifts to us. Look at how much you have to be thankful for! You are a scientist and have recently completed some magnificent work. And you are a classical piano concert master, Alla, and there is certainly a career waiting for you somewhere, but you must make yourself known to those who need you.

For instance, there is opportunity for you to be playing in lounges and hotel dining rooms or at conventions as accompaniment for other classical musicians, small groups, and so on. You need an agent. My daughter is an actress in your city, and all her work comes through an agent. Teaching students, as you are presently doing, is also a good source of work. It may not be what you want, but it is a good start and may evolve into something rewarding. Students may be demanding at times, but it will change things if you give thanks for every student you have as they arrive each day. It will put you in a receptive frame of mind, it will bless them, and their parents will talk about you. You never know where your miracle will come from. Perhaps you could send out more professional brochures to hotels and convention planners and put your beautiful face on the cover. You must take advantage of all your gifts.

Clay, it is evident that you are depressed and down on yourself, and it is understandable. No one with a mind like yours wants to be idle. You certainly need work, and it will come to you. But you must invite it to you. Try to focus positively on the world that has given you the great opportunity that you have just completed in Russia, working out their complicated environmental issues, and picture yourself doing that somewhere else. Like Alla, you must do something other than visit a headhunter and wait for the phone to ring. Perhaps you also could prepare some personal promotions about yourself and get in touch with civic leaders. You may not get a whole country next time, but there are cities that need cleaning up, and the environment is a hot topic. It is important that you continue to play an active role in this process. You may be surprised at what shows up.

Do some small thing each day. To help you overcome the feeling of being "unemployed," perhaps you could find a needy group who would welcome your expertise or some of your other skills and perform volunteer work as a counselor or something else. Important things happen in strange places.

You need to adopt a professional image in terms of your appearance. I would advise you to dress yourself every morning looking as though you could go to work in a moment's notice. The day I met you, your appearance reflected that you are down on yourself, and that compounds how far down you might go. Confidence diminishes, and when you look at yourself in the mirror, you won't like what you see. Alla looked so gorgeous that day. If she had been wearing a sweat suit, I would not have believed that your wife was a concert pianist, nor would I have gone in the car with you.

You must not let this advice offend you. Simply accept it as part of the training for your next commission, and it's free! It is no reflection on who you really are, but as you know, packaging creates the first impression. You need to look like a couple to everyone, especially to yourselves. You are a handsome young man, Clay, and you should be thankful for that. It's unfair, but good-looking people move more freely than others, so you are fortunate indeed. Just imagine: what if in that singular moment when I asked to sit at your table, I were instead the mayor of Halifax visiting Toronto for a conference to find an environmental expert. I may not have paid attention to you because you did not look the part.

Now, above all else, I urge you to pray. It unites you with the universe and attracts to you those things you wish for and, more importantly, those things you need.

This I know for sure. God placed each of us on this earth with a unique gift, in a unique human, like no other. It is our responsibility to use our gifts to enhance the lives of others and to do so with a loving heart. It is easy enough to love one another, but we must also approach strangers with a loving attitude. And we must experience gratitude for our unique gifts.

I encourage you when you awaken each morning to say a prayer of gratitude for all that you have—simple things like food, shelter, warmth, and safety, as well as others like a loving spouse, companionship, friendships, and your extraordinary intelligence. Then pray for the help you need and be specific. Ask for the courage to strike out into the public domain to present yourself. Pray for the wisdom to do it appropriately and effectively. Pray for the patience to get through each day while you wait for results and rewards. Pray for one another in all that you see and need. But *do* pray. There *is* a God, and he is always available.

My husband is a wonderful example of what I have just suggested to you. He and I have each experienced individual successes on a large scale. We were each well known for our individual achievements. We have traveled and spoken to large audiences across the country and have experienced financial comfort. Within one year, we each lost our businesses through no fault of our own. We each encountered corruption in a cruel way from public figures and business partners, causing us to lose everything. We lost our savings, investments, homes, and cars. We felt that we might die from the sense of helplessness, anger, and despair. However, we decided to live, and we decided to live well. We got up every morning with the belief that we could change things, although we didn't know how. We did not know how to begin, so we prayed. We prayed separately and quietly during all our waking hours.

My husband found work on the bottom rung of a ladder he had previously climbed. Each morning he shaved and groomed; pressed his suit, white shirt, and tie; and went into his office in our house, where he did whatever he could to begin a new life. No one saw him there but me. Nevertheless, he dressed as though he were already where he wanted to be. He never altered that habit. He stood up to talk on the phone; he never lounged in a chair. He stood tall, and he walked his usual gait. Standing made him feel strong and in control.

Each day I dressed, did my hair and makeup, wore attractive clothes, and walked somewhere. We had no money for bus fare. I often walked six to ten miles a day. We didn't have the privilege of having coffee in a café or seeing a movie in the theater. We began to pray aloud together. This served to keep us united and of one mind. My husband heard my pleas, and I heard his. We bonded in a powerful way and remain so to this day, many years later.

We have arrived at a place in our lives where we are well, confident, peaceful, optimistic, and full of love for one another and most of those we meet. We laugh together and play together and talk about everything. We are afraid of nothing because we know how to pray. We have no qualities that do not already lie in you. You need only to awaken them.

I know nothing of your beliefs. If they are weak, develop them. If prayer is uncomfortable for you, just get started. Do something every day that makes life different from yesterday. Our lives here are abundant with miracles. Find a church to attend. Church congregations are simply people like you and me searching for answers and life-changing opportunities. It develops a sense of belonging. Shop around until you find where you belong. Somewhere there are two seats waiting for you.

Thank you for sharing a moment of your life, for taking me in, and for trusting me. I shall be forever grateful. I have a meditation tape in the making. I trust it will enrich your life. I will continue to pray for you.

Marie

7
Betrayal and Healing

Dear Amy,

Just now, driving home from town, a letter to you started to write itself. I have been waiting for nearly a year for one to happen. You know, of course, that I wouldn't write anything without praying first. I have been praying all this time, and nothing appeared. But while driving up the lake road a few minutes ago, I had some lovely music on, and a string orchestra was playing "Wind Beneath My Wings." Strangely, my eyes filled with tears. This is my song for my sweet husband, and I offered a quick prayer of gratitude for this wonderful man in my life. The next song was "Feelings," and for some reason, this letter began. I parked the car, went straight to my computer, and wrote without ceasing. I am sending it to you as it came to me.

Last evening, Ian and I shared a meal with you and Adam in our home. We have not been seeing one another socially as we once did, and I wanted us to eat together here this one time before you set off on another cruise. I had two goals: to get a sense of how you would be with me and, more importantly, to reaffirm for Adam that we care about him and will do anything for him and remind him that we live only down the road.

Last Christmas season was when you shocked my life, and I hurt in a terrible way for a long time. I wept and wept with deep hurt. I was very confused at my own depth of feeling over your behavior. I knew it was deliberate, and I knew I had reason to be hurt but not so deeply.

These were the cumulative events. I reconstruct them for you in the hope that as an old friend you will switch places with me; place yourself in my shoes, as it were. We had been experiencing your declining interest in our Friday night evenings together only to discover that you were calling our old friends while excluding us.

You will recall that weeks before Christmas you invited us to spend Christmas evening supper with you for "some leftovers and a glass of wine." We had already been invited to a nice Christmas dinner with some old friends, but there were already ten of them and only the two of you, so we declined their invitation. We felt a loyalty to you as our old friends, and you were going to be alone at Christmas.

I called to invite you to one of our several Christmas parties. When I gave you the date, you said you would have to look at your calendar and that you were about to take a shower and would call back. More than two hours passed. I felt a huge knot in my solar plexus. Consider, if you will, that this is scarcely something to be upset about, but for no apparent reason, I could feel an intense negative energy. So I called you. You reminded me in curt tones that you said you would call back but that you were not free because you had invited our old friends for the weekend and would all be busy. I did think it odd that you could not remember before the shower that you had guests for the weekend. However, then you added, scarcely drawing a breath, that all of your nights were booked up including Christmas evening, which you intended to "spend quietly at home, just the two of us, which is just the way we want it." I felt as though I had been kicked in the ribs, and I understood that this was a pivotal moment. I was overwhelmed with confusion, and finally, thankfully, anger. Anger spares us from inappropriate grief. Thankfully for us, our old invitation was restored, and the other couple was delighted to have us. Twelve of us enjoyed a grand old Victorian Christmas dinner in an idyllic environment.

I could not do that to anyone—and I mean anyone. I certainly could not do it to a friend. I couldn't even do it to someone I dislike. I needed to understand why you were deliberately cruel. Almost a year has passed. It took me six months to get some answers. All my answers came as a result of prayer. I prayed day and night. I simply had to be free of the hurt and confusion. You know how I find solutions. I have shared a great deal of my inner self with you, especially in the first few years of our friendship.

In my spiritually enlightened moments, I observe more and more that when one is being attacked, the Lord reaches out his hand and sorts it all out. I was praying, and I was trusting for answers. Now, after all is said and done, I am content and at peace.

You have said some inaccurate things to mutual acquaintances related to our distant relationship, but no harm has been done to any of us—except you, of course. You are hurting yourself, and while it is none of my business now, it concerns me. As an old and caring friend, I believe you should examine your motives. "The truth will find us out." More importantly, "The truth will set us free."

Several comments from last evening's conversation indicate that you are not free. You are bound up in some competition of your own creation to claim the friends of others as your own, and you have been doing this for some time. Wanting new friends is natural and healthy. And we ought to share our friends. We cannot, however, just order them up. They blossom from small seeds into lovely things for a long time, a lifetime, or a short time. We can't make them happen. When we give love just for the sheer joy of it, we please God, and he rewards us tenfold.

I loved you, Amy. I still do. Love doesn't just get handed out when things are okay and yanked back when they turn sour. The relationship has changed, as you have noticed. I have no idea whatsoever how you feel about me. I know now that you never loved me, or you could not have behaved as you have.

I needed to be free of the pain generated by your actions and couldn't understand, actually, why it mattered so much to me. So I prayed, and I prayed. One day last summer on a brilliant sunny day, I was walking down the hill toward the lake praying out loud. (I actually scared a local gardener!) "Lord, show me why I am hurting so much. Tell me why I am letting Amy be so important in my life. Why am I feeling so much pain? It doesn't make sense to me. Lord, help me." I was repeating this plea, and just as I got to the lake, a distinct, male voice said to me in my right ear: "Because you want her to love you. You don't need her to love you. I love you." Then I knew. I had never outgrown the little girl

27

who needed the women in her life to return her love. It had started with my mother. My mother is a whole book. I have forgiven her and have come to love her in a wonderful way since her death.

Now I am free and have been since that day. But you are not free. You have huge burdens, and they seem to be of your own making. We talked once of the seven deadly sins: lust, gluttony, greed, wrath (anger), pride, sloth (laziness), and envy. Which ones are we committing during some or most of our waking hours? Do we eat more than we need? Do we crave more worldly goods? Whom do we envy? It is not my place to tell you how you need to change. I have challenges of my own. When we were close and talked, I was always open with you about my own walk, and I shared all that I understood. If you are ever to find inner peace, you must place your life in the hands of God and ask where he wants you to be, how he wants you to be, and how you can learn to love those whom you resent.

This is where the freedom lies.

I wish that for you—freedom and peace.

Marie

8
Ye of Little Faith

Dear Bill,

Out of the blue in the car today, some phrase or word on a tape clearly brought to my mind a story I wrote called "The Magic Carrot," and something came to me that you are like that little boy who planted a seed and knew instinctively that a carrot would grow.

I realize that second to your wife, gardening is probably your greatest passion. I thought how ironic it was that you, Bill, of all people want proof in order to believe that there is a greater power. Don't you see? You already believe!

You told Ian and me that you have already put lots of seeds in pots in your basement preparing for the day when they can go into the ground. You do this every year, do you not? You do this with the absolute faith that without any doubt whatsoever, one moment on a warm summer day in your garden you will be looking at cucumbers, peas, beans, and carrots of your very own that have been growing down there in the dark.

Like the little boy who planted one carrot seed, you have no proof, but you have faith, and that faith is so secure that you spend hours watering, weeding, pruning, and loving every moment because you "know" what is happening beneath. You are engaging in the making of miracles! Of course, you don't do this all by yourself. Some force/

power provides rain, soil, warmth, sun, and, yes, two loving hands and a joyful heart.

You want proof! What proof do you have that your seeds will produce sprouts and that those sprouts will become something wonderful down there? Honey, down there—that's God. God is power. God is everywhere. That is why our idyllic weekend was idyllic. It is a miracle that we four are together as a harmonious group. Think of the age ranges, the backgrounds, the childhoods, and the diverse personalities. This is no accident. I believe we are placed with the right people at the right time to learn from and to serve one another.

Plant something else, Bill. You are a teacher. Plant a good idea in one student's head and watch it grow. How do you know which one will come to something? The greater the need, the greater the act if done with love, the greater the result, the greater the miracle when one simply moves in faith. There are only two conditions—faith and fear. If you were afraid that all those good seeds would just do nothing, you would do nothing.

All the rest—all the other miracles—happen when we keep acting in faith. Trying. Risking. Believing in an idea or a person. Sticking with a problem until there is a solution—that's faith.

Why do some of us read the Bible? Why read anything? To accumulate information—to be stimulated, entertained, advised, and informed. And why all that? To be more comfortable, comforting, interesting, fun, productive, and helpful to others. Get a new piece of information, and if it works, we share it right away. That's why some of us read the Bible.

It is packed with advice; accounts of failures and successes; challenges and triumphs; and rules for living a joyous, peaceful, healthy, and rewarding life. It is all things—history, rules, advice, promises, and encouragement. Internationally, it has been the best seller for generations.

Many people shy away from reading it. I asked Ian (my husband) why he thought that was. He said he thought it was for the same reason that many people don't go to church. They think it is full of rules they will have to obey and that they will have to change their lifestyles. You and your wife are already living by most of the rules.

The first half of the Bible is a history of certain parts of the world before Christ was born and how life was then. People did awful things to one another, but there were also very wise men with gifts of prophesy who predicted that a boy-child would be born in a certain unusual place and would grow up to change how we think and behave toward one another. Good thing.

This boy became a teenager and then a young man, and extraordinary things began to happen around him. He said some profound and exciting things to people with problems. He did some unbelievable things, so we are told. The New Testament is all about what happened after he appeared and what his admirers said he did. He was quoted, attested to, loved, respected, reviled, and feared—just like you and me. You've got followers. I just know you do, and I'll bet my chocolate cookie they trade stories about what you do and say, and then those people pass it on to someone else, and so on, and they are emulating you without realizing their source. Later, this man was destroyed by his enemies. Sounds like last night's news, but there is more to it than just that.

Why not read it and discover exciting pieces of wisdom and comfort that can affect your life in a big way? The early translations are difficult to read, but more recent editions use modern language, and there are some good stories in there. Some people claim it is not "totally accurate," but where can you find the absolute truth about anything? In the media? From a friend? From your wife? Anything you hear from these sources comes with their own interpretation. Big deal. In the Bible, the essence is intact, and the advice is foolproof.

When I hit a glitch in my day and find myself growing from distressed to distraught, I just sit, close my eyes, and pray to that "power" (the one that makes vegetables grow in your garden from mysterious little seed) to help me clarify my thoughts and create some order in my head. I need to understand why I am upset, and then I ask for guidance to overcome it. I could call a friend to confide and discuss; I could get bad advice. I could turn on some music to drown out my thoughts, but they will return eventually. I don't have the patience for that, so I sit quietly and pray and wait for some measure of truth to move into my head. Now I know from experience that it will. I get answers in an hour, a minute, tomorrow—but I do get answers.

For example: After weeks and months of hurt and confusion created by my old "friend" Amy, after buckets of tears and prayers and no relief, one day I was walking and praying aloud. "Tell me why I am hurting so much. Why is this ordinary person creating so much pain in my heart?" A voice in my right ear said: "Because you want her to love you. You don't need her to love you. I love you." There it was—a lifetime of advice. God loves me.

I knew right away that was the answer. I don't need her to love me. I thought I did, and so I allowed her to treat me badly, to use me. That's all gone now. How quickly it was resolved. We all want to be loved. I had just added her to my list, and in my desire to have her love me, I permitted behavior that was hurtful and cruel, and while I would feel awful at times, I wasn't quite clear why. It just sat in my middle like a cold lump. When I tapped into the power, I got the solution.

We understand that God is love. There is either love, or there is fear. There is nothing else. I would like you to examine these ideas and give me an argument.

Now I will let you go. Thanks for listening.

Just one more thing; I must tell you this. I was reminded of why sometimes when we pray it feels as though we are praying to the clouds. Listening to a tape in the car on the way home from our lovely weekend, Ian and I were reminded that successful prayers need certain elements. That is, to connect to this universal power, we must also contribute to it. Whatever we give out we get back.

First when I pray, I confess to any thoughts or things I have done during the day that I am not proud of, and I ask for forgiveness. This puts me in touch with those things in me that I need to work on—things that are intruding on my peace of mind. Then I give thanks for all the great and tiny things that have happened on that day that changed me or gave me pleasure or peace. This helps me to feel full and fortunate—grateful instead of deprived. Then I ask for whatever help I want, because now I am honest with this universal energy/power/God.

That's it. I hope some of this is useful or at least interesting.

Much love,

Marie

9

Speak Love

Dear Daughter,

You light up my life! You are like a candle in the corner of my heart. Being with you is always a unique experience. You fill me with joy and pride and, finally, peace. I had an idyllic few days with you. It was so good to have some hours not shared with others to learn more things about one another.

I love that you have achieved tranquility and have developed a peaceful environment in which to live.

I love the way you use your mind to learn new things and your desire to share them with others.

I love that you are interested in enriching the lives of other women, and you desire to help them to make good choices.

I love the way you care for your body to keep it healthy and beautiful, and it is both. I feel joy when I look at you, because although you are my adult daughter, you are still my precious little girl.

I love your sense of humor.

I love your creativity and the results.

I love and admire your willingness to listen to the counsel of others and your receptiveness to mine, even if you do not always agree. It makes me feel free. When you use my ideas, it makes me feel valued and important.

I believe you are on the brink of something big. Big doesn't necessarily mean fame. It could be doing well on this planet and serving others. It doesn't always mean wealth, but then it could be any of the above and more.

I pray for you every night between ten o'clock and midnight and often again in the morning as I awaken. I offer my gratitude and ask for protection for you.

I thank God that you are an important part of my life. I thank you for sharing your wonderful self with me.

Devotedly,

Mom

10
Infidelity? Save Your Marriage

Dear Kate,

I feel such intense hurt for you right now and the pain that has invaded your lives. I don't wish to seem mysterious, but I believe there is a negative energy in your household that is growing because it is in some way being nurtured. I say this because I know that when we foster a good energy, it grows and grows, and life can become a magical thing.

I believe good energy is God and God at work. You can neither do yourself harm nor create any confusion if you tap into the power that is God, whatever you believe him to be. I have a lifetime of proof on a daily, sometimes hourly, basis that when I dwell on the good things in my life, I see my horizons widening and opportunities for pleasure and happiness appearing. It comes in many forms. Sometimes I just look out the window, and some new delight appears, like a purple finch; or the phone rings, and it is an old friend with good news; or I am throwing out old magazines when an article catches my attention, and it is precisely what I need to know that very moment.

As my husband says, "What we think about, we bring about." And you think your husband has been unfaithful.

When the world turns its ass upside down, I need to kick it into position right away and make a plan. I need to make a plan, beginning with how I want things to be. I need to decide the first thing that needs to be done—some small thing to begin the turning around, something within my own ability, within my own power. If we are going to start with speaking our minds to our partners, we need to prepare the words. They need to be clear, without apology, and positive. In the darkest moments, we need to believe on some level that no matter how bad it looks there is an opportunity for a light to shine. If you don't have a bright light, at least light a candle! We must not turn out the lights and live in darkness. Without truth, darkness is left. We must seek the truth. When there are two of us, we seek it together.

When two people are in crisis, one is always stronger. No matter how unfair, that person has to fly the plane. I often feel that I have been the pilot most of my life and frequently resented it. But now I am being rewarded tenfold. I used to wonder why it always had to be me. Now I know it was because I was the fittest most of the time. That's the way the earth keeps its balance. Those who are the most sober have to drive the car. Those who can still bend over have to clean the floor. Those with the best voices get to sing the arias. Those who grow beautiful gardens get to be admired. You must relate to that. The rest of us just mow the lawns and take out the garbage.

We each fit some place just right at some time. Sometimes the right place feels like the wrong place, but whoever is the fittest has to lead. Between you and your husband, I am sure you each recognize who is the fittest right now. Make a plan—first to speak and then what to say. Begin with one small clear thing that you know you want. Is he in agreement? Find out what else you agree on. Do you want to spend the "golden" years together? How do you each perceive them? What do you have in common in your individual plans? At this stage, it is all about security and contentment. And it is only about one day at a time. Year by year isn't there after the middle years. Half the opportunity has flowed by; the other half is waiting for the plan. Financial focus is not so crucial. You got this far, right? Now the focus is pleasure, satisfaction, growth, health, and companionship.

I am speaking, of course, about my life, which I believe is mostly like everyone else's. When you get a big health threat, the picture becomes clearer, and the plan is refined. You carry it out a day, or a week, at a time. Much beyond that is just too ambitious. However, the benefit of this thinking is that one learns to live consciously, to live in the moment, and any moment can become a treasure. You notice the good stuff and absorb less of the detritus.

There is one strong overriding ingredient in the success of this, and it is prayer. I would have accomplished nothing beyond daily survival after my horrendous business losses had I not engaged in prayer. I prayed day and night. I prayed in the car, riding the ferry, and walking to the store. I prayed at the kitchen sink, at the stove, and in bed. I prayed short but fervent prayers. I believed there was a God. I had not even arrived at Jesus Christ as my source. I believed there was a God because as a child I prayed for help when I was being abused by other children, and I was protected from harm against serious odds. I have come a long way.

Now I am a practicing Christian. That means that I have read the stories of the life of Jesus, I believe them, and I subscribe absolutely to following his beliefs and his advice. When I am faced with a serious decision or a sense of abandonment, I go straight to prayer. I pray wherever I am. I pray sitting, standing, walking, driving, or lying down, whether in public or in private. I am trying to say that I do not believe there is a rule for praying or that any one way is superior to another.

I have learned that supplication, surrender, humility, and contrition are all a means to full contact with the Holy Spirit. I must leave my earthly angers, fears, unforgivingness, and frustrations behind. I must "fall on my knees," at least figuratively, to receive the benefits of the guidance and wisdom that has only one source.

I believe absolutely in the validity of the Holy Spirit. Why not? I believe that the spirit of my deceased baby daughter lives. I believe that the spirit of my mother lives. Yes, I believe that the spirit of Jesus lives, that he crosses miles, races, and countries, and that he is available to all of us all of the time.

When I pray deeply with a desire for clarity, I wait until I can feel his presence, and I ask for the help I need. I believe that he deserves my praise and my gratitude, so I acknowledge who he is and what he has done. I express gratitude for the blessings in my life in detail. In expressing gratitude, I have a heightened sense of how much good I have in my life, and my problems diminish by contrast. Unless we identify our blessings regularly, we take them for granted and wish for something to satisfy a longing that we may have created ourselves.

I am sharing this with you because you know I pray, and I tell you that my prayers are answered. They are not always the answers I hoped for, but they are always perfect. When I tell you I will pray for you, I do. In fact, this letter is the result of prayer, and I am moved to write just as I have done. After you called, I prayed for you periodically through the day, each night just before sleep, and again each morning upon awakening. This letter began in my head one morning and again this morning, so I am writing as it comes through me. It is early in the day. I am still in my night clothes, but the message is strong.

It is important to know in your spirit and your heart what or whom you are praying to and to believe that you are being heard and will be answered. That is simply an act of faith. There seems to be no tangible proof (although I believe there is), so it is difficult for the scientific and questioning mind. But tell me this: what is there to lose? There just might be a lot to gain.

You may wish to share this letter with your husband. I would urge you both to pray and indeed to pray together. One other powerful aspect of prayer is to confess your sins and ask for forgiveness, and then as a move toward healing, promise yourself to change. Some people do not think they are sinners. I used to wonder about that myself, and then I began to recognize where I needed to change. The scripture names seven deadly sins: gluttony, greed, lust, envy, sloth, anger, and pride. We all commit them sometimes, and they are soul destroying. I know now when I am acting in sin—that is, acting wrongly. I feel that knot of warning deep in my solar plexus.

Ian and I went through rough times to hold our marriage together, particularly at the beginning—too many single years, so many experiences, and so many fears. If we had not begun praying, we might have said to hell with it; it's too much work. Not only did we agree that we would pray for our individual struggles in the relationship, but we also agreed to pray for the welfare of the other person. So we began to share those things for which we needed prayer. Then we began to pray together out loud while sitting together and holding hands. We still do that. We prayed for one another—for wisdom, courage, patience, and insight. We prayed for our children, our friends, our neighbors, and anyone who asked us for help. I also know that group prayer works in a powerful way. I believe that if you had groups praying for you, you would begin to feel something shifting in your lives.

When I was going through the open-heart surgery, there were at least two hundred people praying for me at our church. All the pastors and staff were praying together in their office. Friends were praying. I was aware of it. When friends used the expression "lift you up in prayer." I had no idea what that meant until that experience. I truly felt lifted, enveloped, and protected. Before I went into surgery, I told Ian that if I came back, I knew I had work to do. So when I awoke from surgery, I knew I was alive for a reason and said, "Well, here I am. I wonder what I am to do."

I am wondering about your husband. Is he feeling useless? Perhaps he is not doing what he is meant to do, and he senses that. Perhaps he does not know what it is, but it makes him feel empty.

Each of us has a different need. I have finally sorted out what mine is, and I am doing my best to serve others accordingly. What other purpose could we have? We all have gifts, and we must have purposes. Viktor Frankl wrote about that in *Man's Search for Meaning*. The survivors of the German prison camps were those who had a reason to go back. Some of us have fame awaiting us. Some of us just work quietly in our own little patch. We each have a place.

Each of us was given a gift unlike anyone else's. We use it to please ourselves and to serve others who need us. That's the whole picture. We are told not to hide our light. We are told to thank God for our gift every day. It changes everything—everything. It allows us to see the quality in our lives and to identify the source of joy and pleasure. Recognizing your gift is vital to opening your eyes to opportunities for creating internal satisfaction.

Likewise, prayer is as vital as breathing. I suspect you pray only when things go wrong. Because if you pray when things are good and pray with gratitude, you will notice more and more things that are blessings in your lives. The list expands, and the other things we see as negative will slowly fade.

I wish for you that this crisis will turn into a challenge that you will meet with all the courage and determination that you have demonstrated all your life. Miracles can happen. I have a history of them, and I am only one drop in the great big sea that has been rescued through the grace of God. Someone once asked me if I am "born again." I replied, "Yes, every morning."

Love from both of us to both of you,

Marie

11
More Things Wrought by Prayer

Dear Carrie,

You are facing some huge challenges, and I have been praying for you. I have a story to tell you that I believe will be meaningful to you. As I write it, I am thrilled all over again.

You are aware that my husband Ian is hearing impaired. In fact, he is legally deaf, and last year a specialist discovered a tumor. Ian had been experiencing a blocked feeling in his ear and thought it was wax. The specialist told him that he would need surgery and that he needed it soon because the tumor would start affecting his brain. We were very frightened. The specialist said he would need to find another surgeon for Ian to see.

As we awaited the call, we prayed to be sent to the right person. We prayed for someone who would relate to Ian as an individual, who would communicate well with him, and who would instill confidence. We had an understanding of what the risks were and thought of nothing else.

We were referred to Dr. David Morris. Moments into our appointment, this attractive young surgeon felt right. Ian, who was born in Blackpool, England, detected a familiar accent. After a brief conversation, Ian discovered that not only was Dr. Morris from the same town in Lancashire, but the two had lived on the same street. Two sets of eyes were sparkling, and we *knew* our first prayers were answered. In a few moments, we heard another familiar accent and discovered that Dr. Morris' assistant also grew up in Burnley. Ian spent his teenage years in Burnley, a beautiful English town.

Ian was a victim of the bombing in Britain during World War II. Overwhelmed by multiple bacteria, his eardrums collapsed when he was three, and he was deaf until age fourteen. Through the years, he underwent three surgeries that restored hearing in one ear and enabled him, with a hearing aid, to have a successful career as a teacher and lecturer. This recent tumor diagnosis made us both very anxious for the ensuing years in terms of his work. Dr. Morris told us that he would expect to have no hearing after the surgery for a period of three to four months. He had only one functioning ear, and that was the ear that was growing the tumor. I began preparing myself for the stress of communicating. I was also concerned that my husband was facing some very intrusive surgery and considerable pain. I felt so helpless. We had been praying for so long and felt confident that the final outcome of the surgery would be successful.

The date for surgery was September 19, and he was coming home September 20. I drove him to the hospital early in the morning and sat with him as long as I could. We reminded one another of our prayers and how confident we were. I went straight home and sat in my "quiet place" where I meditated on the confidence we felt and our good fortune in finding just the right surgeon. Charlie Brown, our adorable shih tzu, paced the hallway, checking the bed for Ian. He knew something was different. He nagged me to let him out. He sat outside in the dark until ten o'clock waiting for Ian to come home.

The following morning two friends brought Ian home from the hospital. I had hand signals rehearsed to express my important thoughts. As he ambled down the walk, leaning on our friends, he spoke to me. I answered him, and he heard me! He had somehow developed hearing in the "bad" ear. We knew we were having a once in a lifetime experience. So many people had been praying for us. Our gratitude was beyond expression. Ian said he could feel the prayers, and so could I.

I share this story with you because you are so far away and are in need of this. We send our love and continue to pray for your protection and comfort. Never give up.

Love,

Marie

12
Love, Sweet Love

Dear Meg and Glenn,

I awoke at 2 o'clock, and you were the center of my attention. Thoughts of you and the boys came floating through my mind, most of which were centered on Meg's ongoing pain and lifestyle challenges. As I lay there, it also became clear to me that not only is her life profoundly affected by her disabilities and pain, but all of you are.

Glenn, I know it must affect you deeply, because I am aware of my sense of responsibility to "fix" Ian when he is unwell and experience such a sense of inadequacy when I cannot. Words of comfort help. Sometimes relief ensues. I have been thinking about that and realize it is an act of love to say comforting things, especially when we don't feel like it. When we extend love to another in times of difficulty, we connect with God for a few moments.

I tried to read myself back to sleep, unsuccessfully. (I keep a stack of uplifting reading material beside my bed.) My thoughts of Meg's pain returned, and I wondered if perhaps she was awake at that very moment—that perhaps we were awake together, and God was trying to speak to both of us through one another. The thoughts were so strong, and then a prayer began to form in my mind. So here I am at my computer in the middle of the night transcribing it for you.

I asked God what he wanted me to do, and I got clear direction that I should get out of bed, write the prayer, send it off to you, and direct you and the boys to say it together out loud just before bedtime. Sit together and hold hands as you pray. (The prayers follow this letter.)

Another prayer is coming through for Megan to say when she is alone in the living room and unable to sleep. I believe that God speaks to us when we are quiet, and I know that we long to hear him most of all when we are quiet and alone. I expect Glenn hears his voice when he is paddling on the river.

We are never completely alone, of course. God is always with us—how comforting. When we feel alone, it is when we have looked away from God. Someone once said that when God seems far away, guess who moved.

I absolutely believe in the power of prayer. I believe it reaches souls on other parts of the earth. I have been praying for years for a wonderful relationship with all my children, and it is now being manifested. I am the most grateful of mothers. I give thanks first thing each morning when I awaken for my children, for my grandchildren, and for Glenn's goodness and loving ways. My blessings multiply each time I hear one of your voices or receive one of your hugs.

So many of my prayers have been answered. Now God is finding work for me to do for others. Use these prayers I send you now. I promise you blessings.

God bless each of you in a special way.

All my love, always,

Mom

A Prayer for the Family

Dear God,

We come to you as a family at this moment because we know you love us and because we love one another. We thank you for all you have done for us today and for all you will do for us tomorrow. We thank you that you have given us one another to live with and to love, and we thank you for the special individual qualities that you have given each of us to share with one another.

We know how much you love us because there is so much love in our home. We are grateful for everything we have with one another and everything you give us each day. We thank you for our ability to do the things we have to do each day.

We come together at this moment to pray for Megan, our mother and wife. We ask your healing hands to restore her to a healthy body so that she may serve you according to your will. We ask, dear Lord, that you show her ways that she may affect changes in lifestyle and thinking that will give her comfort and confidence. We pray that you bless this family with wisdom and peace. We thank you in advance for all the blessings you have planned for us and for the wonderful life that we are already given. Amen.

A Prayer for Megan

Dear God,

I come to you alone in this quiet room at this quiet time to hear your voice. I have been awakened by pain, and I feel lonely and helpless at these hours because I seem unable to help myself. I know you love me, and I know you will help. I pray at this time that you reveal to me why this is happening and what your plan is for me. I thank you for those times of relief when I can do those things I enjoy, and I thank you for the strength you give me to endure the pain when it comes.

Lord, I ask that you help me to feel freedom from discouragement and show me new ways of healing. I thank you for all the blessings in my life and for so many people who love me, care about my welfare, and look after me in special ways. Lord, I ask for healing so that I may also look after them and others you place in my path. Show me how to lead a more productive life, according to your will, and give me the strength and ability to do what you would have me do.

I place my body and my thinking in your hands and pray that I will be receptive to you in every way. I thank you for all the blessings in my life, and I now rest in you. Amen.

13
Surviving in a Divided Family and Learning to Love Again

My Dear Children,

Today is Mother's Day, and we are thousands of miles apart. I would give anything to have all three of you here together with me this day. I am so glad to be your mother. You are so different from one another and each wonderful in your own way.

Ian bought me flowers today to celebrate—three roses, one for each of you. We went to church and then to lunch in a quaint town for pastries and coffee. I felt truly treasured and indulged. We are very happy together. I wanted you to know that. Your mother has finally found her mate. It was a long search—one I had given up on. We met under unusual circumstances—in a bar. Neither of us goes to bars or ever had. We both understood clearly that lonely people should stay out of bars. You meet the wrong people there and develop dangerous, destructive habits.

I had been praying for the Lord to send me the partner I needed because I had chosen so poorly in the past. I asked for whomever he thought would enhance my life in a positive way and decided I would cease looking. And I had. So I did not recognize him when my prayers were answered. We liked one another when we were introduced and knew we had something in common. However, we simultaneously divulged that we would never again marry; we would just be friends. Our friendship was based on those things we had in common: work ethics, drive, goals, ideals, dreams, and spiritual beliefs. We had different reading and recreational habits and different tastes in music, sports, and entertainment. We had disagreements. We often separated. We always came back because we knew we should. That was twenty-six years ago. On my next birthday, I will be eighty years of age.

Let me tell you what has held us together. We want to share this with you because it changes lives.

We share the same ideals to live in harmony with one's mate and also one's fellow man; to share beautiful experiences and beautiful things with someone of value; to be totally honest with one another at all costs.

We have learned to openly express all our feelings—our happy ones, our hurting ones, our fears, and our triumphs, both large and small. We have learned to take personal responsibility for things that go wrong, even losing our tempers, rather than blaming the other. We are still growing and still working at learning how to live good lives. Above all, we each have always had and continue to have now a deep, abiding faith in God. This is the foundation that built this wonderful relationship, brought it together in the first place, and kept restoring it when it became weak.

One cannot turn back the clock. The father you had was the one who gave me you three wonderful children. I would not change that. But this I know: if I had been brought up in a Christian home, I might have saved that marriage. It takes two, of course, but the knowledge and love of God would have led us on far different paths, which eventually had us living apart and depriving you of the stability of two parents who respected and loved one another.

I cannot change what happened when you were children. We will always carry scars, but we do outgrow much of our hurts as we grow in other ways and as we understand, exercise compassion, and forgive. I have had a lifetime of learning to understand my mother and to forgive. It was in the terrible hurting days of my childhood that I discovered God.

I remember clearly. On one of those awful days when my parents were shouting at one another, I ran back to the apple orchard. I was running away from home again. I threw myself on the ground under an apple tree and wept my little heart out. I lay there looking up at the sky and the interesting shapes of the clouds while absorbing the comfort of the warm grass. I felt a soft peace envelop me; I felt it was love, and I believed it was God and that I was being taken care of.

There was another awakening. I was sent away to school to live with my aunt and uncle. They had eight children. I still do not know why I was sent away. Imagine shipping an eleven-year-old away from home with no explanation to live with people who do not love her. I remember certain things like being sent to bed before it got dark in a room by myself where I was not allowed to read. They would banish me when they had special treats like making popcorn. They would all sit around at mealtime at a huge dining table together, but I was seated at the other end of the kitchen to eat with a black man who worked for them. I knew what the implications were, but I did not understand why they did not like me. I learned to love that lovely man; he was the only kind person there. His name was Henry. He knew clearly why I was required to sit with him, and I received love from him. How ironic.

My first days at the school were terrifying. I had no one to walk with. The kids threw stones wrapped in snowballs at me and taunted me. I prayed, saying the Lord's Prayer over and over. I felt protection, and I knew God was there. I have always had that quiet internal reassurance when the world was spinning too fast for me. When I let go of that, I feel out of control. I have to remember every day that there is a divine power and that my life is still in the planning.

This life of mine has been eventful, to say the least. Think of it: at age thirty-eight I lost my life's belongings and home through a fire that was set by a careless smoker; one of my daughters suffered severe burns at age nine, and a baby daughter died. Then there were the divorces. At age 64, my life's work, my business college, and everything I owned was gone—my savings, my home, my career—and all through no fault of my own. One ruthless politician set me up for his own personal gains. Then Ian had to overcome the frustration of losing another business from which we had a debt of sixty thousand dollars—again, through no fault of his own. An innocent man was lied to by a colleague he trusted.

We were certainly tested. Now these few years later, we have recovered. We have a nice home and a place in Florida. We have a car that works. Above all, we have you, one another, and caring friends. We could not have survived this with any sanity or health without absolute faith that God is watching over us and taking us where he wants us to be. It is clear that we are being led to do his work.

We pray that you, too, will find such fulfillment. Every one of us will have trauma in our lives, and there must be a way to relieve the burden through prayer and faith that there is a power greater than in our small selves who keeps order and resolution.

Ian and I pray together daily. We pray aloud so that each knows what is in the heart of the other. We give thanks for all that we have. We recognize how blessed we are every time we sit down to eat. I do not pray for things. I pray always for wisdom so that I might do the right thing in tough times. I pray for courage, which I seem to have lots of sometimes and none at all at other times. And I pray for patience. Every day a small miracle happens.

I hope you will teach your children to pray so that they will appeal to their higher selves when there are big decisions to be made. Daily, life is fraught with challenges and obstacles. I know of no more powerful way to ease fear, pain, or anger than to talk to God and know that without any doubt that he has been listening. I have wisdom and insight beyond my own limitations.

You may wonder why I have chosen this time to write to you in this fashion. Four Sundays in a row, while sitting in church, I got a clear direction to tell my children about myself and this part of my life.

You all know how much I love you. At least, I hope you do. I am proud of every one of you. I love you just as you are. Having children of your own must give you some sense of how I feel about you and how precious you are.

Days fly by at this stage in my life. Some of my friends are preparing to leave this planet. Who knows when my day will be? I am in no hurry, I can tell you, but I am ready. I have lots yet to do and see and experience, and I expect I will be working until I leave. "I have promises to keep and miles to walk before I sleep." (Robert Frost) This time I have left must be top quality. I want you to know me. I don't want you wondering years later what I might have been like had you known me better.

Through prayer, I have become forgiving and compassionate. I have no negative emotions to overcome. I do not know what the future brings, but whatever it is, I feel safe. There is nothing so great that it cannot be overcome through prayer. Pray a lot. Give thanks regularly throughout your day, wherever you are, and you will feel the magnitude of the good things that might otherwise have gone unnoticed. Pray for help in moments of stress and wait quietly. The help will come, often in strange and wonderful ways. Pray for wisdom. We make mistakes because there are things we do not know.

I know God blesses you. I have only to look at what you've become.

My love always,

Mom

14
Search for Joy

My Dear New Family,

Guess what! The sun is shining here back home. Not that I take any credit for that, but I sure am grateful.

It was a short visit but very eventful. The highlight, of course, was that absolutely wonderful evening with all the brothers and sisters at a table together, eating, making a lot of noise, laughing, and seeing your dad smile. I thank all of you for making me feel part of your family. That is important to me. We thank all of you for sharing your home, your time, and your delicious cooking.

We had some delightful visits with old friends and new ones that included long talks and more good food. It was a truly memorable occasion and has probably changed a lot of lives already. It seems your mother's death has been the process that brought everyone together—the first time all of you have sat in a room together and laughed out loud at the dinner table. This could be the beginning of something very exciting. All is not perfect, and there are still some hurts to be healed and some forgiving to do. The forgiving is important.

I have had to do a lot of it. I can tell you that the subjects of my forgiveness have never known and have not changed, but I have. I am grateful to have come to understand the process and would like to share it with you. It takes time and dedication. Egos have to be put aside, and a loving attitude needs to enter.

Ian and I, individually and together, have climbed some mountains through broken marriages and the loss of our businesses and life's savings. We are proud of ourselves now. Prayer has been a powerful force in our lives. It has resolved every hurt, every fear. It has brought us peace, confidence, and happiness. No matter how grim the future looks at any time for any reason, we are comforted by the results of our prayers. If you are not accustomed to prayer or even thinking of God as a solution to your problems, let me share this.

One of my favorite writers is Alan Cohen. My favorite book of his is The Dragon Doesn't Live Here Anymore. (The dragon is fear, disappointment, bitterness, anger, and so on.) He suggested that even if there were no God, the universe could flourish on the foundation of truth alone, and that if it is difficult to accept the idea of God, then pursue truth with all of your heart and mind and you will find fulfillment. He said clearly that the lessons of truth are the lessons of God.

Ian and I are in search of the truth every day. We question everything and everyone. That may sound nervous to you. Nope—we're just careful and wise. We used to trust everyone, giving them the benefit of the doubt until they proved to be dishonest, but that caused us years of grief and profound financial losses, not to mention broken relationships.

Not only do we question others now, but we also check ourselves: Is this really the way things are? Or is it the way we would like them to be? Is he telling the truth, or do I believe because I like what I hear? Am I pretending to be something or someone I am not because it impresses others?

I don't ask for the approval of others or ask them what they think about me. I look for the truth in myself. There's a spot in my middle— my solar plexus—that gets tight and feels bad; sometimes it just feels awful. I think that's where the soul resides. We talk about "having a gut feeling" or feeling really good "inside ourselves." We talk about "not having the heart" for something. You've all experienced it. You know what I'm talking about. I trust that now. It's fear—a warning. "Pay attention," it says. If I'm expected to act on something or respond to someone and I have that warning feeling, I do nothing. If I have that "dark" feeling in the presence of someone, I know things are not right with them. If I have it on my own, I know something in me needs attention. I pray for clarity.

As for my own truth, I do my best to get as close to it as I can, knowing what I know. I try not to pretend about anything. I have no secrets, and Ian and I have no secrets from one another. If I am struggling with my thinking, I pray. I believe with all my heart with every fiber of my being that there is a divine power, an absolute power, a God of all things, a Holy Spirit. I believe because I have so much proof. My prayers are always answered. Always. The answer is not always what I expect, but there is always an answer, or at least some advice. It comes in many forms. Sometimes it's just a thought that keeps repeating in my head. Other times it's a phone call at just the right time, a dream, or an encounter with just the right person at just the right moment.

You have all been answers to my prayers. All of you! Think of it! How wonderful that is. When our prayers are answered, we always give thanks. Expressing gratitude confirms in your heart that you have something valuable. Being thankful elevates your emotions. It reduces self-pity. Self-pity confirms in us the belief that there is nothing we can do and that we are really badly off. Self-pity destroys hope.

Oprah, with her celebrity status, has done some good work among us. One of the things she got people started on was a gratitude journal. I think it arose from Sarah Ban Breathnach, the writer of *Simple Abundance*, a wonderful spiritually motivated book. You write five things every day for which you are grateful—both big things and small things. Thank you for this adorable dog, for coffee with my friend, for a car that started, for a good book, for an affordable load of groceries. You need to find five new things each day. Can you imagine the change in attitude with 150 different things acknowledged with gratitude each month—1,800 new things a year. Wouldn't that change how we view life? It works. It works for me.

When we lost our businesses and savings a few years ago, we had to think creatively every waking moment, or we would have just wallowed in our hard times and wound up on social assistance. We agreed to work together and to talk to one another about everything we were feeling. When one was down, the other propped up. It was so hard. We got strength through prayer, just assuming we were being heard somewhere in the universe. We found comfort in attending church, listening to the stirring music, and hearing a good message that often seemed to speak especially to us. We were so needy, you see, that we were really listening.

The crisis changed our lives. We grew up. We learned what things were of real value: our relationship, good friends, and family. Everything else was just "stuff." Money is still only money, nothing more. It still burns in a fire. It changes value every day. It buys relief, but it does not buy happiness. And the loss of it does not deprive one of happiness. We prayed all the time—for courage, patience, determination, and wisdom. We did not want to make any more mistakes. All our prayers were answered. We became strong and wise and determined, and eventually, we became patient. Now we are afraid of nothing.

If you do not pray already, I hope you will learn to do so. It can change your life in a most remarkable way. People find healing through prayer, both emotionally and physically. Pray for one another. It heals the one who is prayed for and the one who prays. Pray for relief from pain and depression. Pray for forgiveness and to be forgiving in all parts of your lives. It will release you and relax you.

God bless all of you,

Marie

15
Mothers and Daughters

My Dear Daughters,

There is this pervasive ache in the solar plexus that has nothing to do with physiology. It is almost as though while it is in the body it is also outside somewhere, just moving inside to attract attention. It comes to me like the ringing of a telephone—that there is something that needs attention so it must come inside where it can be felt.

But there is relief. Sometimes walking helps; it stimulates positive and creative thinking. Some of my most exciting discoveries happen in my head when I am walking, swimming, or just moving forward. Even in a passive mode, such as sitting on a plane or driving in a car, my creative forces gain momentum when I am moving forward. It seems there is a symbolic connection between moving forward in one's body and moving forward in one's mind. While sitting on a plane or car, I am often interrupted from my daydreaming into some creative thoughts. I carry a notepad at all times so I can record my thoughts while they are fresh in my mind.

There was a time when that ache would send me to a diversion, whether it be reading, talking on the phone, or cleaning frantically. Now I choose to sit with the sensation until I have some sense of what is stirring. Of course, this is facilitated by prayer.

What is stirring today seems to be that I am attempting to relieve my adult daughters' stress by bearing it for them, and it is making me heavy hearted. I am bright enough to know it doesn't work that way. We just double the quantity of experienced pain. I must pass it back to them with the prayer that God will stand behind them and catch them when they fall. I pray that they will feel surrounded by love and light and that I will share whatever I have.

My own life has been so peppered with trauma that I seem to be just healing from the vestiges of one when another begins. I hoped that my girls would be spared. It looks as though we all get our own. So I must remember that I have passed on some of my survival systems and that you are as strong, courageous, and creative as I am and that your pain will strengthen and enlighten you. Would I deprive you of these gifts? No. You deserve them. Then I ask: do you deserve the pain? Perhaps.

Perhaps pain is earned as pleasure is earned. The pleasure is the reward for enduring the pain with courage and integrity. The pain is an opportunity to work through to further pleasure—even ecstasy. Would I rob my children of ecstasy? Never. Then I must leave them to their pain while I offer the warmth of my arms.

And that takes some growing up for the grown-up.

So, my darlings, your mother prays for your journey to be fulfilling— an experience of God's grace.

Sweet love to you this day,

Mom

16
Overcoming Pain

My Sweet Girl,

I know you are struggling with both pride and the toll your pain takes on your general sense of well-being. I need to resist the desire to just keep telling you how wonderful you are and how much I love you and instead to give you more than that. I believe you still have the promise of doing useful and productive things with your life. You have the intelligence, the personality, and (when you are well) the energy. The pain has caused depression, and you spiral downward. So much physical pain is exacerbated by the fear that it will get worse, and then it does. I speak from my own experience. I hope you realize I never throw "stuff" your way just to cheer you. I always try to tell the truth as I know it.

After my heart surgery I was frightened to find myself lying in bed, overwhelmed by pain, and feeling helpless because I was unable to sit up without assistance or reach the phone because I was not permitted to use my arms. I needed to call for help for everything—even getting to a standing position. Then when I got to my feet, I keeled over and was even more frightened. The day nurses felt it was the morphine, so I went off that and onto codeine, which was no better. I went from codeine to something else, and the nausea was overwhelming. We set up children's room monitors, so Ian could hear me in his office if I called. I was otherwise alone.

As I lay there by myself, I, of course, prayed for solutions. I asked for courage, tolerance, patience, and whatever else I needed. I had intense pain, but I realized it would reach a height and go no further. While the pain awakened me, I did not take the drugs, because I got the distinct sense that the courage I asked for had appeared, and I was to try "working through the pain" a moment at a time until I understood what I could bear. So I collaborated with Ian, and we agreed that I would try the no-drug solution, keep the speaker nearby, and call for drugs if I needed something, but only if it became intolerable. We both prayed. Then I went twenty-four hours with intense pain, but I experienced it in a different way and understood that the pain would not kill me. I sat outside myself and watched Marie lying quietly, relaxing, breathing deeply, and "managing." It gave me the strength to take a huge leap of faith, and so I began another twenty-four-hour cycle without the aid of drugs. I just had to know the worst, but I felt such serenity and trust, and so another day passed where I endured pain and lived to talk about it. I never took the drugs again.

This is a very difficult time for you and for your family. Still, I bet my best earrings that you will learn something wonderful through your experience that will be life changing for you or for someone else through you. The scripture is full of promises about that—bearing pain with faith that God is doing a work in us so that we can serve others.

When I lost my Halifax Business Academy, my life's savings, and my special paintings and antiques, the emotional pain was beyond description, but it drove me to prayer. There was nowhere else to go. There was the anger, the frustration, the fear, and the sense of helplessness. I felt like smashing windows, hitting the people who hid from me, screaming at those who did not understand, and fighting with my good husband. But I did none of those things, because my brain was still functioning, and there was something changing in me. There was an angel following me around.

Eventually, I got outdoors, because I couldn't breathe in the house. I walked and walked and walked. I walked to the bus stop (because I also lost my car). I couldn't wait for the bus, so I walked to my destination. I walked up to six miles a day. I had to sell something to buy walking boots. While I walked, I prayed out loud—sometimes coherent prayers of petition and sometimes old church service prayers, the Lord's Prayer, or the twenty-third Psalm. *Tell me what I can do. Show me how to be free. Let me not make mistakes. Show me how to forgive. Help me to be free of anger. Show me how to have new courage. Tell me what you want me to do with my life. What am I to learn from this?* Answers came in curious ways—meeting someone by coincidence who said just the right thing, finding an article in a magazine, seeing an interview on TV, or hearing a message in the sermon at church that seemed to have been put together just for me.

There were ten years of change, growth, healing, and forgiving. Now I have a perfect life. I have a partner who is kind, loving, and productive. I have children whom I can love and be proud of and who love and respect me; I have a sweet house on a sweet property with birds and flowers; I have friends I can trust and some acquaintances I like a lot. I am peaceful and quiet in myself. I am proud of myself and like whom I have become. We have all the cash we need and promises of some just for fun.

In my walking and praying, I discovered the joy that came from offering thanks for every tiny improvement in my life. Whenever I began to pray for help, I first gave thanks. Later I learned to ask for forgiveness for anything that I had done knowingly or unknowingly to offend God or any living person. Then it would be revealed to me how I needed to make things right with anyone I might have wronged or anything that I might not have carried out in a proper way. So it was through the difficulties that I began to clearly see my life's role.

Your dedication to focusing on the wonderful woman that you are and looking to a higher power to lead you will show you your life's role. I will continue to pray for you as always. You are my last prayer at night and my first in the morning. Get well. Be good to yourself. Love yourself the way you would love your child.

We love you always,

Mom

17
Mothers Are Supposed to Love Us

Dear Mother,

This is strange, certainly, but it must be done. It is a letter that will not get beyond the page, for you are beyond the clouds, while I am still in body and full of things to say to you that not only couldn't I say but didn't understand while you were here to listen. I trust you are in a place where you know all things and see all things and that this will reach you on some level.

Now that I am almost the age you were when you departed this planet, I know some important things. I heard myself talking to your granddaughter the other day, and I sounded just like you. I said something to her that you would have said to me and that I would have found irritating. It shocked me, and then it struck me as really funny, and we both laughed. I said to my daughter, "Beware. It's on the way!"

I so much wanted a sweet relationship with you. I never knew how you felt about me. It just seemed to me that you were always critical. I spent most of my life trying to please you and internally begging for a compliment or a tiny flicker of praise. I just wanted so much for you to love me, to hold me in your arms, to whisper sweet loving things to me, and to make me feel that I was valuable in your life. It never happened. Then you left that letter in your top drawer for me to read right after you passed away. You reminded me where to find it several times, so I knew it was important. I hoped that it was words of love that you didn't have the courage to speak. Little did I know—I wept for years. You confirmed what I had always suspected—that I was a disappointment to you in every way. And I had tried so hard.

I understood that you considered divorce disgraceful and were in contempt that I had one, remarried, and then years later divorced again. The element of disgrace was founded, it seemed, on the fear of what people might think.

Much of your advice to me was based on that—*what will people think?* The only conversation we ever had about "sex" was that I shouldn't indulge until I got married, because I might get pregnant and "What would people think?" My virginity was never linked to my spiritual development. It was connected to, and to be punished by, those imaginary "people." Well, I learned the hard way. Don't we all? I married, still a virgin, but too soon and with no knowledge of the married relationship, because I just wanted to be held and hear "I love you" from someone. A cute guy, a great dancer, and a good kisser said those words early in the relationship, and I was hooked. I lived to hear him say it again. But this letter isn't about our marriage. That's another letter.

There was the need to have you find me attractive and pay me just one compliment. I dressed with great care for my visits with you, hoping. But there was criticism. There was criticism about my housekeeping, my parenting, my friendships, my attitude, and my appearance. I cleaned ferociously before your visits. I pretended to change, hoping to please you. But it never happened.

Then I became an admired public figure with a career. I was respected by the community, my colleagues, and my students. I developed beautiful friendships and lovely relationships. People loved me. They told me so and why. I realized I was actually lovable and probably had been all along. I looked at my baby pictures and saw an adorable little girl. I saw that I was holding hands with my mother. I began to sense things were perhaps not as they seemed.

One Mother's Day, when you were eight-six years old, we knelt together in church for prayer. I felt an enormous overwhelming tenderness and love for you. I realized that I had very little time to put us together. That morning, I committed myself to learning how to love you unconditionally and to abandon my own needs that were not to be fulfilled. I was sixty-one, a grandmother, a senior citizen, and a successful professional, and I was still longing for my mother to love me. I knew it would not happen; it was too late. But I needed to love you no matter how you were to me. That moment was the beginning of a commitment to prayer for you—for us. I prayed all my spare waking moments—waiting for sleep at night, getting up in the morning, passing idle moments during the day, eating lunch and dinner, and commuting to work in the car. Nothing dramatic seemed to be coming, but I could feel a change in myself. I began to feel compassion.

One morning I awoke at 4:00 AM with a film playing in my head. It was you and I interacting—like little vignettes of moments together. I saw you, and I saw me. There was language. It started to repeat. I leapt out of bed, headed for the kitchen table, grabbed an old empty scribbler and a pen, and began to write. It was noon when I finished, drained but exultant. I just wrote the words as they were flowing without any involvement of my own. I knew God was answering my prayers. In other words, this was what I read back to myself.

I was told that you needed mothering—that you had never had a real mother and that you didn't know certain things. I was told to mother you, to love you, and to be consistent. You exhaled your last breath at 1:00 AM three years later, three hours after I left your hospital room. I remember clearly my need to be told just once before you left that you loved me.

Then there was the letter in the top drawer—so humbling. And there was the memorial service. You were laid out in that funeral parlor, wearing all the regalia from your lodge years and looking good. Everyone said so. Then someone said how much I would miss you and how much you loved me. I blurted out, "She did? She never told me." There was a long line of visitors. Several heard the exchange and were horrified.

It was so difficult, that emptiness.

So I prayed and prayed. I prayed to understand my own pain and what seemed to be your indifference to me, your little girl. I had little girls, and I could never adequately describe how much I loved them or my little boy. Soon they were adults, and I still loved them in every way. How could you have not loved me?

No shower broke in my head with everything I needed to know. It was just that I seemed to keep running into opportunities that enlightened me and reminded me of all your admirable and valuable qualities—all the things I learned and all the ways I learned to be that got me through the difficult and challenging life that awaited me. You taught me perseverance—to never, never give up. If something didn't work out to just keep trying, especially if it had a worthy result. You taught me the value of hard work and that it really didn't hurt anyone. You taught me to shun self-pity. You taught me courage—to do whatever I was required to do without giving in to fear. You taught me to tackle whatever needed to be done instead of waiting for someone else to do it for me. You taught me how to look after myself, how to cook, how to eat, how to clean, and how to keep order.

You gave me the skills to face my terrible times, to rise up, and to carry on. You taught me how to be groomed and well turned out. (But you never told me I was pretty.)

So I am grateful to you, for it is from you and because of you that I became the woman I grew to love and respect. I was well armed. I learned about the wonderful you through prayer and conversation. As I related my life over the years with friends, often describing you to them, I saw you more clearly and understood how fortunate I was to have been adopted into your life. The alternative would have been too dreadful. I see now that was your kind of love. I was loved after all.

God's blessings on you, Mother. I will always thank you for being you, and I look for you in the heavens on bright nights, because I believe you are a star. Your name is Stella, after all.

Marie

18
You Don't Need to "Diet"

Hi Honey,

I just wanted to share some meandering thoughts following our conversation last evening.

One of my favorite quotes comes from Robert Frost: "Two roads diverged in a wood, and I—I took the one less traveled by, / And that has made all the difference." The one less traveled has other people on it, so it is not lonely. They will speak your language and be attracted to you. I will be one of your co-travelers.

I prayed about this, of course, and so I learned some things. One is that when I need to make changes in my eating habits, they work best if I don't share them and don't talk about them all the time—like, "I started a diet yesterday, so I can't have any of that." There are too many detractors and people with issues of their own who don't want to be disturbed. Just go about it quietly, enjoying it with God and maybe a best friend who really loves you and will feel joy in your successes. There are no failures here, only trials. Every day is new. Every hour is new. And every minute is a second chance.

Let's create some new habits. Habits love doing the same things again and again. Remember the one where you always had a piece of chocolate after dinner? Eventually, it grew to be three pieces, not four or two, but three, and it felt just right. So, try this for a new habit that will grow in you with pleasure and anticipation.

Find a favorite spot in your home where you most like to sit for watching television, reading, talking on the phone, or listening to music. Keep it free from clutter. First thing in the morning, find a few minutes there for a short prayer for your day. Keep it simple, and do it at the same time every morning. Every evening in the same spot, at the same time say a short prayer out loud and then go into the quiet. Just meditate. Allow your thoughts to flow like a river where they just drift on by, no solutions. Create a beautiful image that will be most natural for you and most peaceful. In your imagination, place yourself there. Yours may be riding your bike in the countryside. Slowly relax your body, beginning at the toes. Work all the way up to your scalp. Sit in your silence until you feel ready to come back. When your whole self has had enough, you will automatically return to awareness. (If you find this too difficult, you could use my CD *Finding Your Quiet Place*.) After you are alert and yet still in that delicious peace, praying aloud, ask for help specifically with certain eating habits and for instructions on foods to avoid and foods to increase. The help will come. I promise you.

Always eat from a beautiful plate, while sitting in a favorite place or your meditation space. Eat slowly. Eat mindfully and consciously. Put your attention into your mouth. Become aware of texture, warmth, and flavor. Give thanks for your food. Always eat with the same attention and diligence as when you lick an ice cream cone. Maintain that attitude until the last morsel. Engage in positive, uplifting thoughts and express gratitude for things in your day that gave you pleasure. Speak aloud so you may hear your own thoughts and so they have substance. They will grow in importance, and you will love yourself for the way you are now thinking.

Acknowledge the beauty and the mystery of the food, where it came from, and what it has become through cooking. I find eggs exciting to think about. They are so mysterious. They are beautiful in shape, colorful inside, delicious, and very interesting in the mouth. Think of the processes of the wheat, the grinding, and the preparation of the bread before it comes to us as toast. Add to that the pungent and delicious coffee, and we have a drink shared by many and an opportunity of pleasure often with a friend. This beauty and mystery of food is what we share at our brunch on Sunday.

Whenever you sit in your favorite chair, loosen your waistband and sit upright so to enhance circulation. Close your eyes. Invite the Holy Spirit to come into your space and wait for him. This will always be real and always be responded to. Miracles will happen.

As you know, I have had ongoing challenges with food. I have resolved all of them through prayer as I ask for help and remain attentive to the voice.

These things I have learned, and I am grateful for my extraordinary health.

My love to you and for you,

Marie

19
Never Give Up

My Dear Meg,

It really helped to talk to you last night and be free of my conflicting emotions about my old friend. I still think of her almost every day, but I don't shed a tear anymore. I don't even long to see her. We had certain things in common, and I treasured them. Small things they were, like sitting at her big window, drinking strange herbal tea, looking at all the little birds and squirrels hopping in front of her window, stroking one of her cats, and watching her heat up some cooking at her quaint counter in her quaint kitchen. I basked in the atmosphere she had created in her old house—rustic smells of other times. Then we swapped stories about the goons in our lives. We laughed a lot, like two teenagers. We felt young together. Then there was the other person she was sometimes— the mean-spirited one who made me feel bad about something almost every time I was with her. I see her now as a phase in my life, a nice one, and as history proves, the pain of the bad memories has faded considerably. I continue to pray for her. That is my balm.

Although you are not of my blood, my sweet daughter, we do have things in common, and the things that worry me most about you are those that I have already hidden inside myself.

You are a wonderful woman. It would be a pleasure to know you if I met you elsewhere. There are a lot of people who would feel that way and some who already do. It is time you get outside the "body Megan" and look on at her, admire her as she deserves, see who she really is, and stop making up stories about what you imagine others think. If your critics are not experts, their words are of no value. I probably love you more deeply than anyone on this earth, because that is how mothers are. I love you unconditionally, yet in spite of that, you find me puzzling, frustrating, disappointing, and the list goes on. The only cure for getting off your treadmill is to stay in touch with God and ask him to describe you to you. Just sit quietly alone and listen until you hear his voice or feel his presence and then enjoy the woman that he loves every minute of every day.

I cannot say I feel your physical pain, because I don't. But I am aware that you are always in pain. I am also aware that you have good days, and I rejoice in those. You are rarely out of my mind. You are always in my heart. I cannot allow myself to dwell on your pain, because then I feel more emotional pain than I want to bear. When that happens, I pray short prayers. So I am praying for you several times a day and no less than twice.

I still think you will come into your own and will one day see a light that will shine on your talents, and you will begin doing something, one thing that will occupy your mind and your emotions and will serve others in a good way. You have so much to give. Please try this exercise: Write a list of all your good qualities, and subtitle them as intelligence, training, manual skills, mental skills, emotional assets, and appearance. Spare nothing. Turn it into a brag sheet. Be honest with yourself. You know the truth. No one else will see it or judge your boastfulness. Put your list in order with the best quality or asset at the beginning and the least at the end. Then go to the top of the list and see a description of yourself. Ask yourself how you would employ this woman if she came to you.

Find a way to earn a living either in your home or out of your home on your own terms according to your ability and availability. I see lots of assets. You have a great phone voice, nice quality, lots of energy, a sense of humor, and interest in talking on the phone. You are also very creative and arty. You are interesting to be with. You are kind. You make people feel good.

Look for the real woman within you and share her with the rest of the world in a way that will fit for you.

May God bless your year.

All my love,

Mom

20
Just Love Him

Dear Sandra,

It is presumptuous of me, perhaps, to write as I do, because I am a new friend in this unique group of women. Nevertheless, I was quite moved by your personal story of your son, your manner, your candor, and your sense of freedom as you shared this delicate information with us. I thank you for that. I wanted to hug you right on the spot.

Your story has been on my mind ever since. You were struggling with what the truth might be for gay men and women as we see it from a scriptural view.

I have had a number of gay friends over the years, both male and female. Most of them seemed comfortable in their lives, and I was comfortable with them, although only one of the couples spoke of their Christian lives. I loved them all, and I understood their loving one another. Our lives have changed, we have all aged, and we have drifted apart for a variety of reasons. I have prayed for all of them over the years, as I do for my friends now. But this week, I found myself praying for answers.

This was left in my heart after your last comment about what the Bible says and how you should view this challenge in your life. So I prayed about it. This is what came back to me.

The Bible is an old book, written a long time ago. Science would not have been, at that time, investigating all the interesting things we are learning about the brain, so they would not have been privy to the information that we now have. That is, those of us who are unusual sexually are wired differently. We have learned some interesting things about Alzheimer's, autism, dyslexia, and so many others. I am not suggesting that I think homosexuality is an illness.

I do know that my gay friends all loved one another in a deep and meaningful way and are together still after all these years. They often reminded me that their relationships lasted longer than my marriages. There are those who practice gay sex who are not respectful or loving and who enter into a different relationship simply to follow their lust. Then there are those lovely people like my friends and your son who are monogamous, who love and respect one another, and who want to spend their lives together. I wish there were a special ceremony written by theologians for those who want to take vows of fidelity, protection, respect, and honesty where they could be celebrated with friends who are happy for them.

I was particularly impressed by your openness and trust in telling your story, and I thank you. You will surely be blessed for this gift to us. I prayed to be led to a group of interesting women. I was starving for intellectual stimulation and time with women. I accidentally learned about you and your group one day while attending a funeral. God always knows where to find us. I'm loving it … and you.

Marie

21
Lost and Found

Dear Laura,

Thank you for lending me your book. I got through most of it. I found it thought provoking. I already had preconceived opinions about much of it, mostly in agreement with the writer. I have done a lot of reading during my lifetime, some useless and some deep and unforgettable. I thank God every day for my eyesight.

Now I have a story to tell you about this book and why it looks as though it has been run over by a two-ton truck. It has. Here we go!

I left your office happy, stimulated, and full of thought, hopped in my car, and headed home. Eager to read the book, I looked over at the passenger's seat, and there was no book in sight. I pulled over on the shoulder, checked the seat, checked under the seat, checked under all the other seats, and then did it all again. I dumped my oversized handbag out three times and looked through everything; I even looked in the trunk, although I knew it couldn't be there. Now my heart was racing, for I had lost my pastor's book, and she needed it for Sunday evening. I turned the car around and drove back to the church, checked every inch of the parking lot, and checked down the hill. Nothing. I returned to the office where Carol confirmed that when I left, the book was under my arm. I was in such a state of anxiety. *What am I going to say to Laura?* So I headed back up Ochterloney and began praying: "Tell me where to look. Tell me what to do." A masculine voice in my right ear said,

"Watch the road." I refocused from distance to the pavement in front of the car, and there it was.

The book! It was in the middle of the road, all the way up Prince Albert past the super store. I stopped right there in that busy intersection, got out, and looked around for cars—not a car in sight. I picked up the book, hugged it to my chest, and loudly exclaimed, "Thank you. Thank you. Thank you." Is this not extraordinary? Again, my life is changed.

Thank you once more for lending me your book. I apologize for the tire marks and the rended binding. I have ordered a new one from Miracles Book Store, which will be here early next week. I will deliver it to you the minute it arrives.

Blessings,

Marie

Note to the readers: We think the book had been laid on the trunk while I packed other things in the car. Laura would not accept a new book. She thought the event was too important. So she taught from the tire-treaded book and told her students what happened.

22
Pray! For Heaven's Sake!

Why do I pray?

To stay centered and focused. To maintain a sense of balance and perspective. To stay calm in moments of fear, confusion, rising irritation, or anger. To stave off the urge to be judgmental of others, thus increasing trust. To rise above self-pity. To subdue fear of the unknown. To reduce feelings of helplessness in times of struggle. To maintain a healthy body and a sense of youth and energy. To increase confidence in the welfare of my family and those I love. To remind myself of the need for humility and at the same time to remind myself of my greatness. To maintain a level of sensitivity so that I may be aware of the light and the darkness.

When do I pray?

All day long, at any moment, and at night whenever I awaken. For a few seconds or for a few minutes—sometimes for hours.

Where do I pray?

Wherever I am at the moment—peeling carrots at the kitchen counter, getting ready to answer the door, waiting at a red light, lying in bed, sitting in the living room, sewing, getting ready to enter a room full of people, waiting for an appointment, sitting, standing, lying down, kneeling, walking, swimming, and driving.

What do I pray for?

Patience, courage, and wisdom. These three qualities seem to influence all my needs. I never pray for wealth or "things." I pray for the wisdom to acquire things I would like to have, if it is God's will. I pray for the courage to act when the time is right. I pray for patience in all matters and that I will wait for God's work to be done in myself and in others on whom I depend for any reasons.

How do I pray?

First, I give thanks for my blessings—those things I have that protect me: basics, food, shelter, warmth, and safety. I also give thanks for my wonderful marriage, for my children, for the love of family and friends, for the opportunities, for the kindnesses, and for the daily miracles. I give thanks each day for another day of living. I give thanks to remind myself how privileged I am and for the experience of feeling gratitude. I ask forgiveness for any sins I have committed, even for those of which I might not be aware. I assume they are forgiven and put them away. I pray aloud whenever I can, which is most of the time. I pray simply, in my own words, from my own heart. I invite the Holy Spirit to be with me to remind me that I am being heard. I pray aloud with others as often as possible. I pray entirely without pride or fear.

Then what?

I try to remain calm and quiet in my head and my emotions so that I will hear God's voice when he speaks to me and so that I may see the opportunities, because I am confident that they are always being presented. I try to keep the window of my mind clean so that I may see the world clearly, as it really is and not as what I have made it to be. I meditate often during the day, meaning that I sit or lie in a comfortable and quiet spot, empty my head of conflict and fussing, and breathe quietly and deeply until I feel healing and serenity.

Marie Watters-Brown

Bibliography

Cohen, Allen. *The Dragon Doesn't Live Here Anymore*. New York, New York: Ballantine Books, 1981

Frost, Robert. *The Road Not Taken*. New York, New York: Henry Holt and Company, 1916

Frankl, Viktor. *Man's Search for Meaning*. Boston, Massachusetts: Beacon Press, 1959

Printed in the United States
by Baker & Taylor Publisher Services

Printed in the United States
by Baker & Taylor Publisher Services